DEBATING WAR AND PEACE

**Books are to be returned on or before
the last date below.**

DEBATING WAR AND PEACE

MEDIA COVERAGE OF U.S. INTERVENTION IN THE POST-VIETNAM ERA

Jonathan Mermin

PRINCETON UNIVERSITY PRESS   PRINCETON, NEW JERSEY

Library of Congress Cataloging-in-Publication Data

Mermin, Jonathan, 1966–
Debating war and peace : media coverage of U.S. intervention
in the post-Vietnam era / Jonathan Mermin.
p.   cm.
Includes bibliographical references and index.
ISBN 0-691-00533-8 (alk. paper). —
ISBN 0-691-00534-6 (pbk. : alk. paper)
1. War in mass media. 2. Mass media—United States.
3. United States—Military policy. 4. United States—
Foreign relations. I. Title.

P96.W352U556   1999
070.4'49355'033073—dc21   98-43564   CIP

For Hannah and Naomi

Contents

Tables

Preface

UNDER THE First Amendment, the press is free to report criticism of the government, and it is often taken for granted that the United States therefore has a press that is independent of the government. But what has been done with the freedom of the press in practice? Have American journalists used their freedom to offer an independent, critical perspective on government policy decisions? Or has the press let the government itself set the terms and boundaries of policy debate in the news? What is it reasonable to expect of the press in pursuit of the First Amendment ideal? These questions are the focus of this book.

In the age of the World Wide Web and the fragmentation of television audiences, and with dozens of political magazines on the market, it is sometimes said that the quality of foreign-policy debate in the *New York Times* and on the evening news does not have the impact on the public sphere it once had. I believe this is flat wrong. The elite media continue to be the major source of information on U.S. foreign policy for Americans, especially those near the middle of the political spectrum who are not the most dedicated observers of public affairs, but who often end up deciding elections. It is true that alternative sources of news and commentary are available to citizens who have the motivation and the resources to track them down. But on questions of foreign policy such citizens are few and far between.

It is nice to have new and alternative media "out there," but before we can conclude that the power of the *New York Times* and the evening news to set the terms and boundaries of debate in the public sphere has passed into history, it has to be established that citizens are in fact "out there" too, engaged with the new media and reacting to their contents. Outside of the interested and engaged few, however, such a scenario—especially in foreign policy—has yet to be realized. The great majority of Americans still get their foreign-policy news from newspapers and television, not from specialized web sites or magazines. It is therefore essential to understand and critique their performance.

I would like to thank some of the people and institutions who helped me with this project. Erin Wright provided exceptional research assistance. The Block Fund at Yale and the MacArthur Foundation offered generous financial support. The material in chapter 6 on Somalia is reprinted with permission from *Political Science Quarterly* 112 (1997): 385–403. Some of the material on critical coverage of the *execution* of U.S.

foreign policy first appeared in *Political Communication* and is reprinted
with permission from Taylor and Francis. I have been fortunate to receive
advice and criticism from Timothy Cook, Bruce Russett, Stephen Skowro-
nek, and two anonymous readers. The manuscript benefited from the fine
editing of Richard Isomaki. And I am grateful to Malcolm Litchfield at
Princeton University Press.

DEBATING WAR AND PEACE

One

Introduction

WHEN THE United States invaded Grenada in 1983, the Reagan administration conducted a campaign to convince the public of the wisdom of its action. In speeches, press conferences, and interviews, administration officials declared that American medical students in Grenada had been in danger, that international Communism had been on the verge of expanding into Grenada and toward the United States, and that democratic rule on the island had to be restored. The situation in Grenada, the White House asserted, justified military intervention.

The Bush administration orchestrated a similar campaign to win support for U.S. intervention in Panama in 1989. The White House argued that Americans in Panama had been in danger, that Panamanian leader Manuel Noriega had to be arrested on drug-trafficking charges, and that democratic rule in Panama had to be restored. The U.S. bombing of Libya in 1986, U.S. intervention to counter the Iraqi invasion of Kuwait in 1990–91, and U.S. intervention in Haiti in 1994 also were the focus of major White House efforts to win public support.

Presidents have good reason to work hard to win public support for their foreign policies.[1] The political damage Harry S Truman and Lyndon B. Johnson sustained when public opinion turned against U.S. intervention in Korea and Vietnam testifies to what is possible when such efforts fail. On domestic issues, the White House is often able to deflect blame for unpopular policies onto the opposition party in Congress. When the president acts as commander in chief of the armed forces, however, there is no confusion about who is responsible. For this reason, presidents are extraordinarily interested in influencing public opinion on questions of war and peace.

Presidents exert this influence through the news media. For citizens who are the object of White House public-relations campaigns, the news media are of great significance, as most Americans get no information on U.S. foreign-policy initiatives except what is reported in the news.[2] Mili-

---

[1] On presidential efforts to shape public opinion, see Samuel Kernell, *Going Public: New Strategies of Presidential Leadership* (Washington, D.C.: Congressional Quarterly Press, 1986); and Jeffrey K. Tulis, *The Rhetorical Presidency* (Princeton, N.J.: Princeton University Press, 1987).

[2] On the agenda-setting power of the media, see Walter Lippmann, *Public Opinion* (New York: Macmillan, 1922); Bernard Cohen, *The Press and Foreign Policy* (Princeton, N.J.:

tary interventions are played out far beyond the experience of most Americans, for whom they are, in effect, media events. In reporting military interventions, therefore, journalists take on one of their greatest responsibilities.

It is clear that the media are players in the construction of foreign-policy debate in the United States. But what part do they play? Do journalists function as independent, critical observers of U.S. foreign policy? Or are presidents able to structure and control media coverage of their foreign-policy initiatives? At stake in this question are matters of constitutional significance, pertaining to the operation in practice of the First Amendment ideal of a press independent of government.

The towering example of Vietnam might seem to indicate that presidents are unable to set the terms and boundaries of foreign-policy debate in the news. Some observers concluded that the media had emerged as independent critics of U.S. foreign policy in the 1960s, reporting the Vietnam War in terms that contradicted the official declarations of the Johnson and Nixon administrations. Journalists were said to have generated public opposition to the war with stories that encouraged Americans to question the wisdom and the credibility of their government.[3]

In the 1980s, however, a counterargument appeared. Daniel C. Hallin found that newspaper and television coverage of U.S. intervention in Vietnam had been very supportive in the early and mid-1960s, when a consensus in Washington supported U.S. policy. Not until 1967–68, when high officials in Washington had spoken out against the war, does the news turn critical. Hallin offered a simple explanation for the emergence of critical coverage of the Vietnam War: mounting opposition to American policy inside the U.S. government. Until critical perspectives on the war had been expressed in Washington, no alternative to the White House position on the nature of the conflict in Vietnam and the need for U.S. intervention could be found (except at the margins) in the news.[4]

In 1990, W. Lance Bennett offered a general formulation of what Hallin described in the Vietnam case. The mainstream media, Bennett argues, " 'index' the range of voices and viewpoints in both news and editorials according to the range of views expressed in mainstream government de-

---

Princeton University Press, 1963); and Shanto Iyengar and Donald R. Kinder, *News That Matters* (Chicago: University of Chicago Press, 1987).

[3] See Peter Braestrup, *Big Story: How the American Press and Television Reported and Interpreted the Crisis of Tet 1968 in Vietnam and Washington* (Boulder, Colo.: Westview Press, 1977); and Martin F. Herz, *The Prestige Press and the Christmas Bombing, 1972: Images and Reality in Vietnam* (Washington, D.C.: Ethics and Public Policy Center, 1980).

[4] Daniel C. Hallin, *The "Uncensored War": The Media and Vietnam* (New York: Oxford University Press, 1986).

bate about a given topic."[5] The spectrum of debate in the news, the indexing hypothesis asserts, is a function of the spectrum of debate in official Washington. If there is debate inside the American government over U.S. policy, critical perspectives appear in the news. If government policy has bipartisan support in Washington, however, critical perspectives expressed outside the government are not well reported. Bennett found that coverage of U.S. aid to the Nicaraguan Contras in the 1980s fit this pattern, with critical coverage of American policy rising and falling in the news as Democratic opposition to Contra aid waxed and waned.[6] I follow Bennett in using the term *indexing* to describe journalism that lets the spectrum of debate in Washington determine the spectrum of debate in the news.

The findings Bennett and Hallin report on Vietnam and Nicaragua illuminate those two cases but do not demonstrate a general pattern. In examining coverage of eight military interventions in the post-Vietnam era—the invasions of Grenada and Panama, the bombing of Libya, the buildup to the Gulf War (divided into its August and November phases), the Gulf War itself, and U.S. intervention in Somalia and Haiti—this study offers systematic evidence of the impact of foreign-policy debate in Washington on the spectrum of foreign-policy debate in the news.

It would be no great surprise to find that the spectrum of debate in the news was *to some degree* indexed to the spectrum of debate inside the government. Conflict inside the government is newsworthy, and one would expect it to be reported. The words of government officials, moreover, often constitute diplomatic events that demand coverage. Evidence that there is a correlation between debate in Washington and the spectrum of viewpoints reported in the news is not, therefore, of such great interest.[7] What would be of great interest is evidence showing that critical perspectives do not just increase from a reasonable baseline in the news when there is debate in Washington, but instead are ignored or marginalized in the news if not first expressed in Washington.

If critical perspectives on policies that win bipartisan support in Washington are simply outweighed or overshadowed in the news by the official perspective—what might be described as the *correlation* version of the in-

[5] W. Lance Bennett, "Toward a Theory of Press-State Relations in the United States," *Journal of Communication* 40 (spring 1990): 106.

[6] Bennett, "Press-State Relations." Bennett also offers evidence of indexing in coverage of the Gulf War; see W. Lance Bennett and Jarol B. Manheim, "Taking the Public by Storm: Information, Cuing, and the Democratic Process in the Gulf Conflict," *Political Communication* 10 (October–December 1993): 331–51.

[7] For evidence of such a correlation, see John Zaller and Dennis Chiu, "Government's Little Helper: U.S. Press Coverage of Foreign Policy Crises, 1945–1991," *Political Communication* 13 (October–December 1996): 385–405.

dexing hypothesis—then indexing is not a matter of much significance. But if critical viewpoints not articulated in Washington are ignored or relegated to the margins of the news—the *marginalization* version of the indexing hypothesis—then this tells us something quite striking about the relationship of American journalistic practice to the First Amendment ideal of a press independent of government.

The First Amendment Ideal

What makes the indexing of debate in the news to the spectrum of debate in Washington an interesting phenomenon, if the evidence supports the marginalization version of the indexing hypothesis, is that it would appear to contradict the First Amendment ideal of a press independent of government. As Supreme Court justice Potter Stewart formulates this much-celebrated ideal, the First Amendment creates "a fourth institution outside the government as an additional check on the three official branches."[8] In the words of Justice Hugo Black, in the First Amendment, "The Government's power to censor the press was abolished so that the press would remain forever free to censure the Government."[9] Although this interpretation of the First Amendment goes well beyond what the founders appear to have intended,[10] the principles Stewart and Black expound are essentially uncontested in the modern era. The press is seen as an independent observer of political power, having the right and the responsibility to maintain its independence of government.

But what precisely is "the Government" in this formulation? In the context of foreign policy it must include—at a minimum—the president and Congress, the executive and legislative branches.[11] This, one might imagine, is what the press is expected to be independent of. If the indexing hypothesis is correct, however, one must conclude that American journalists report the news, in practice, as if the *president* were the government, and critics of U.S. policy inside the government—in Congress or within the administration itself—constituted an independent vantage point. When spelled out in these terms the premise sounds absurd. But this is how journalists in effect operate under the indexing rule.

[8] Quoted in Lee C. Bollinger, *Images of a Free Press* (Chicago: University of Chicago Press, 1991), p. 177, n. 44.
[9] Quoted in Nat Hentoff, *The First Freedom: The Tumultuous History of Free Speech in America* (New York: Delacorte Press, 1980), p. 206.
[10] Timothy W. Gleason, *The Watchdog Concept: The Press and the Courts in Nineteenth-Century America* (Ames: Iowa State University Press, 1990).
[11] In some cases the judicial branch also comes into play, although on foreign policy this is relatively unusual.

Under the indexing rule, the press is independent of the *president*, but not the *government*, as it does not offer critical analysis of White House policy decisions unless actors inside the government (most often in Congress) have done so first. This means the media act, for the most part, as a vehicle for government officials to criticize each other, reporting criticism of U.S. policy that has been expressed inside the government, but declining to report critical perspectives expressed outside of Washington. In this role journalists perform a necessary service, but not the more demanding one that liberal interpretations of the First Amendment assign.

It is often just assumed that the First Amendment ideal is fulfilled in the United States. In formal legal terms, the American media *are* independent of government, free to report the news without official interference. But if the evidence shows that journalists are letting actors inside the government set the terms and boundaries of foreign-policy debate in the news, then the free press is voluntarily surrendering to the government an essential element of its power under the First Amendment. Under these circumstances the press would be failing to play its full part in the constitutional system.

This failure is not just a problem for idealists. If a consensus inside the government—as often exists on foreign policy—could be interpreted as clear evidence of the wisdom of government policy, the journalism just described might not be a matter of great concern in practice, as a Washington consensus could be assumed to represent the public interest. But what if a Washington consensus is best interpreted as a *political* phenomenon, one that could be tied only tenuously to public preferences and assessments of the public interest? I argue in chapter 2 that consensus inside the government is often the outcome of strategic political calculations that put some issues and alternatives on the Washington agenda and push others off, for reasons that often have more to do with the strategic interests of politicians than the substantive merits of policies. Opposition party politicians, in other words, often have powerful strategic incentives not to speak out against a White House decision, whatever their evaluation of its merits. It is therefore not reasonable for journalists to assume—as the indexing rule appears to do—that if there are legitimate grounds for questioning a White House decision, the questions are going to be articulated in Washington debate.

If the spectrum of Washington debate is a political phenomenon that is often not well connected to reasoned evaluations of the public interest, then the failure of the press to maintain its independence of Washington debate has disturbing implications for U.S. foreign policy. The effect of foreign-policy news indexed to debate in Washington, I argue in chapter 7, is to maximize the impact of the imperatives of domestic politics on foreign-policy debate in the United States. Much of U.S. foreign policy in the twentieth century has been based—in principle if not in practice—on the classical realist ideal that sound foreign policies are the outcome of the deliberations of enlightened statesmen, attuned to the national interest and free of extraneous domestic influences. But journalism that indexes foreign-policy debate in the news to the spectrum of debate in Washington enables a factor that realists see as extraneous to sound foreign policy— domestic politics—to set the terms and boundaries of debate in the public sphere.[12]

One might imagine that independent, critical media coverage would be a domestic influence on foreign policy at odds with the realist ideal. But my own conclusion is just the opposite. Journalism that granted increased coverage to actors outside of Washington, who are free of the incentive to engage in the much-derided behavior of "playing politics with foreign policy," would in fact *reduce* the impact of domestic politics on foreign-policy debate, and might encourage the formulation of more enlightened and realistic foreign policies. Evidence supporting the indexing hypothesis, in other words, is *not* evidence against the impact of domestic factors on foreign policy. On the contrary, it indicates that the media operate in a manner that encourages presidents to react to domestic political imperatives, instead of focusing on the realities of the international environment, in setting the nation's course.

Critical Reporting

There is something puzzling about the indexing hypothesis as formulated up to this point. American journalists believe they are more than just chroniclers of official words and deeds, and politicians experience the news as a critical force, not as an instrument of state propaganda.[13] But the indexing hypothesis would seem to suggest that when official sources are in consensus, "the media play a relatively passive role and generally reinforce official power to manage public opinion."[14] How could journalists— with their commitment to independence of government enshrined in the First Amendment and their often-noted "streak of hostility toward the

---

[12] On the idea of the public sphere, see Daniel C. Hallin, *We Keep America on Top of the World: Television Journalism and the Public Sphere* (London: Routledge, 1994), pp. 2–10.

[13] On the self-image of American journalists, see David H. Weaver and G. Cleveland Wilhoit, *The American Journalist: A Portrait of U.S. News People and Their Work* (Bloomington: Indiana University Press, 1986), pp. 112–17.

[14] Hallin, *America on Top*, p. 11.

holders of political power"[15]—be content just to report the perspective of a united government? When there is consensus in Washington, what does the press do to create the impression that it is fulfilling the First Amendment ideal?

In her influential study of "objectivity" as a journalistic practice, Tuchman argues that reporters stake a claim to objectivity through the presentation of "conflicting possibilities."[16] She illustrates this with an example of a foreign-policy situation on which Democrats and Republicans offer conflicting views.[17] The appearance of objectivity is achieved by reporting "both sides" of the story, the Democratic and Republican positions.

But what if official sources are united on one side of the issue? When there is no policy debate in Washington, journalists find "conflicting possibilities" not in the wisdom and justification of U.S. policy itself, but in the *execution* and *outcome* of U.S. policy, and the possibility of political triumph or disaster for the president. When there is no policy debate in Washington, reporters offer critical analysis *inside the terms of the Washington consensus*, finding a critical angle in the possibility that existing policy, on its own terms, might not work. As the government is often personified in foreign-policy news in the figure of the president, questions about the ability of the government to achieve its goals are often framed as political questions: Will the president emerge as an effective leader, or sustain political damage? When there is consensus in Washington, the media are vigilant for signs that the president is not achieving the goals he has set, and for the possible political fallout if his policy does not work as designed. In this manner, the media avoid confronting the gap between principle and practice that the indexing rule appears to produce.

Seeing the critical angle that *is* found in the news when official actors are united helps to explain the conviction of journalists that they offer independent, critical coverage, and the experience of politicians that the media are an adversarial force. This should dispel the impression that evidence supporting the indexing hypothesis means that American journalists are mere propagandists for the state. But the parameters of the independent critical reporting journalists do offer are quite narrow.

If a policy does not work on its own terms, this is certainly evidence that the policy is flawed. Yet a policy that is well executed and does work as designed is not necessarily a sound one: consider U.S. support for the

---

[15] Ibid., p. 7. See also Thomas E. Patterson, *Out of Order* (New York: Vintage Books, 1994).

[16] Gaye Tuchman, "Objectivity as Strategic Ritual: An Examination of Newsmen's Notions of Objectivity," *American Journal of Sociology* 77 (1972): 676.

[17] Ibid., pp. 665–66.

shah of Iran and the Somoza regime in Nicaragua, successful policies on
their own terms for decades before their sudden failure in the 1970s.[18]
The performance of a policy on its own terms is essential information, but
just one element of what citizens need in order to assess the decision
that set it.

There are some general standards for democratic foreign-policy debate
that an independent press might be expected to observe. U.S. policy itself—not just its execution and the political implications for the president—should be the subject of critical analysis. The basic objectives being
pursued should be examined, to ensure that Americans are in a position
to evaluate U.S. policy on terms independent of those the president
has set.

In addition to the ends of U.S. policy, the means that have been selected
to secure U.S. objectives should be assessed. In cases of military intervention, is the use of force the best course of action? Or could less violent
means produce the desired result? To judge the wisdom of a policy, citizens
must be in a position to evaluate it in the context of potential alternatives.
The choices should not be framed as existing policy or inaction, as this
misrepresents the true context in which decisions are made and casts an
aura of inevitability around the specific action the president has taken.

The relationship of declared objectives to true objectives should also be
examined. Are the stated goals of U.S. policy in fact the real ones? In an
age where "spin" is a major White House output and public relations a
presidential preoccupation, it does not require a conspiratorial cast of
mind to see that the relationship of official justifications to the real motiva-
tions behind U.S. policy needs to be established, not just assumed.

These criteria for democratic foreign-policy debate might seem uncon-
troversial in principle. But the evidence in this book shows that the basic
elements of debate just described are not present in the media unless politicians and government officials themselves have conducted a debate that
includes them.

The debate journalists do conduct on their own initiative, although it
presents conflicting possibilities vis-à-vis the execution and outcome of
U.S. policy and the political fate of the president, creates a powerful sense
of inevitability about the policy itself. It frames government policy as if it
had been stipulated at the outset, finding conflicting possibilities in its
outcome, as opposed to framing government policy as open to critical
analysis and debate, the product of choices among conflicting possibilities.

[18] On Iran, see James A. Bill, *The Eagle and the Lion: The Tragedy of American-Iranian Relations* (New Haven, Conn.: Yale University Press, 1988). On Nicaragua, see Robert A. Pastor, *Condemned to Repetition: The United States and Nicaragua* (Princeton, N.J.: Princeton University Press, 1987).

Critical analysis of the president's ability to achieve his own objectives, I argue in chapters 3 and 4, positions the reader/viewer as a *spectator* to the military operation and the political game, in a position to speculate on its outcome, not as a *citizen* with the tools to deliberate on the soundness of the decision to conduct this operation, to make this move in the political game, in the first place. If the quality of foreign-policy debate in the news—and the positioning of the reader/viewer as spectator or citizen—is a function of the quality of foreign-policy debate in Washington, the independence of the press must be questioned.

Independent Journalism

If the ideal of a press independent of government demands that journalists not relegate independent critical analysis to the execution and outcome of government policies and the political implications for the president, but also examine the wisdom and justification of the decisions that set those policies, how is this ideal to be achieved when official actors are in consensus? Others have offered vague or impractical prescriptions, instructing journalists to strike a more critical posture toward government or to maximize the diversity of perspectives in the news. Instead of arguing for a change in the orientation of reporters toward their sources, or the impractical rule that journalists grant universal access to their pages and programs, I suggest a simple procedure that could enable journalists to better achieve the ideal of independence with relatively modest adjustments to existing journalistic practice.

In addition to official sources, foreign-policy experts and ordinary citizens sometimes appear in the news. But most of the foreign-policy experts journalists consult are figures operating in or near Washington policymaking circles, where the influence of a consensus inside the government is great. Ordinary citizens are most often consulted through mass opinion polls and "person-on-the-street" interviews, where the impact of opinions expressed in Washington and reported in the news is powerful. I argue in chapter 2 that if journalists expanded their definition of foreign-policy experts to encompass those operating inside *and outside* of Washington, and expanded their definition of the public to encompass the mass public *and citizens who manifest a real interest and engagement in U.S. foreign policy*—and who are therefore less inclined to mirror a Washington consensus—the power of official actors to set the terms and boundaries of foreign-policy debate in the media could be reduced. I examine the impact this could have had in two of the Washington consensus cases, the Panama invasion (chapter 3) and the deployment of U.S. troops to Saudi Arabia in August 1990 (chapter 4).

Contrary to the prescriptions of "public journalism," I do not suggest that journalists increase their reliance on mass opinion polls.[19] When military intervention wins bipartisan support in Washington, the polls register strong support for U.S. policy.[20] But students of public opinion have established that such polls are not independent of Washington debate, but to a great extent reflect that debate (see chapter 2). Public journalism, despite its promise in the area of election coverage, is not the solution to the problem described in this book.

Testing the Indexing Hypothesis

Chapters 3, 4, and 5 test the indexing hypothesis in eight cases of U.S. military intervention in the post-Vietnam era. In four of the cases U.S. intervention won bipartisan support in Washington; in the other four cases U.S. intervention generated conflict in Washington.[21] The four *Washington consensus* cases are the bombing of Libya in April 1986; the invasion of Panama in December 1989; the deployment of U.S. troops to Saudi Arabia in August 1990; and the Gulf War in January 1991. The four *Washington conflict* cases are the invasion of Grenada in 1983; the doubling of the American deployment in Saudi Arabia in November 1990; the raid on a faction hostile to U.S. forces in Somalia in October 1993 that constituted the decisive turning point in the U.S. intervention in Somalia; and U.S. intervention in Haiti in September 1994. I excluded cases such as the Iran hostage rescue mission in 1980 and the deployment of U.S. marines to Lebanon in 1982, where reaction in Washington was ambiguous, neither overwhelmingly supportive nor substantially critical. The independent variable in the study—reaction to U.S. policy inside the government—is therefore a simple dichotomous variable: conflict or consensus.

The news media I examine are the *New York Times* (news and opinion sections), the most influential newspaper in the United States; ABC's *World News Tonight,* a leading evening newscast; and the *MacNeil/Lehrer Newshour,* the program generally thought to offer the most in-depth coverage and the greatest diversity of viewpoints on television. The *New York Times,* beyond the impact it has on its own elite readership, influences the foreign-policy coverage of other American newspapers as well, because

[19] On public journalism, see Jay Rosen, *Getting the Connections Right: Public Journalism and the Troubles in the Press* (New York: Twentieth Century Fund, 1996).

[20] Richard A. Brody, *Assessing the President: The Media, Elite Opinion, and Public Support* (Stanford, Calif.: Stanford University Press, 1991).

[21] I used *Congressional Quarterly Weekly Report* to determine the reaction of the opposition party to U.S. intervention.

reporters and editors often look to the *New York Times* for cues in deciding what constitutes news and how to report it. As Graber puts it, "In the political news field the *New York Times* is the lion whom the jackals follow."[22] The impact of the *New York Times* on what other papers report is at its height in the area of foreign policy.[23] The *New York Times*, moreover, is a relatively liberal paper, one that might have been expected to offer *more* critical coverage of military interventions under Reagan and Bush than other leading papers. For these reasons, if critical perspectives on Republican interventions are marginalized in the *New York Times*, it is likely that they are marginalized in other newspapers too.

As there is no evidence of significant variation across the three evening news programs,[24] *World News Tonight* should be representative of television news in general. The *MacNeil/Lehrer Newshour*, however, like the *New York Times*, offers an especially challenging test of the indexing hypothesis. If this program, one believed to include a relatively wide spectrum of sources and viewpoints, marginalizes critical perspectives on U.S. intervention that are not first articulated in Washington, this is powerful evidence in support of the indexing hypothesis.

The focus of the analysis is on critical viewpoints not attributed to foreign sources. This is because foreign critics of U.S. foreign policy do not have much credibility to an American audience. Foreign critics, as a rule, do not phrase arguments in terms that speak to American interests or concerns and often argue in ways that are bound to strike Americans as outrageous, irrational, or simply bizarre. For example, as Americans debated the costs and benefits of going to war against Iraq in the fall of 1990, Iraq and its foreign supporters issued statements about holy wars and imperialism that bore no relation to the terms of debate in the United States. In the case of demonized enemies, the impact of foreign criticism may even be to *increase* support for American foreign policy in the United States. Brody argues that "criticism by our adversaries will make it harder for Americans to express negative views and thus symbolically make common cause with our enemies."[25] Jordan and Page find that foreign critics— even those from allied nations—have no impact on American public opin-

---

[22] Doris A. Graber, *Mass Media and American Politics* (Washington, D.C.: Congressional Quarterly Press, 1989), p. 48.

[23] Ibid., p. 330.

[24] For evidence that foreign-affairs coverage on the three evening news programs is quite similar, see James F. Larson, *Television's Window on the World: International Affairs Coverage on the U.S. Networks* (Norwood, N.J.: Ablex, 1984).

[25] Richard A. Brody, "Crisis, War, and Public Opinion: The Media and Public Support for the President," in *Taken by Storm: The Media, Public Opinion, and U.S. Foreign Policy in the Gulf War,* ed. W. Lance Bennett and David L. Paletz (Chicago: University of Chicago Press, 1994), p. 219.

ion.[26] Offered the choice of an *American* position and a *foreign* position, most Americans prefer to be on the American side. The figures in this study, therefore, are (except as noted) for critical viewpoints not attributed to foreign sources, for editorials and columns written by U.S. authors, and for opinions expressed by Americans on the *MacNeil/Lehrer Newshour*.

"Evidence supporting the indexing hypothesis," Bennett writes, "would suggest that the news industry has ceded to government the tasks of policing itself and striking the democratic balance."[27] But this conclusion requires evidence to support the marginalization version of the indexing hypothesis, not just the correlation version. Instead of establishing a fixed numerical definition of marginalization, I examine the coverage in two mutually reinforcing ways. One form of evidence is quantitative, the results of a simple content analysis (described in chapter 3) designed to measure critical perspectives on U.S. policy in the news. A second form of evidence is based on a close reading of the coverage, designed to offer a tangible sense of the volume and character of critical reporting.

Exceptions to the Rule

The prediction is that indexing is a general rule in media coverage of U.S. intervention, not a universal law. In addition to establishing the rule, I expect to encounter some exceptions. One way critical perspectives might get into the news despite a Washington consensus is if mass demonstrations against U.S. intervention are reported. As Gitlin has argued, demonstrations have news value because of the conflict and social deviance manifested in them.[28] Gitlin shows, however, that journalists tend to frame antiwar demonstrations in terms that undermine their message, focusing on the element of conflict and deviance, often at the expense of real discussion of the issues behind the protest.

One expects to see coverage of mass demonstrations—if their size is great enough to impress journalists—in the news section and on the evening news. On the opinion pages and *MacNeil/Lehrer*, however, mass demonstrations should not have much impact. Demonstrations are reported because they are thought to be interesting stories, not because journalists believe their participants to be credible sources of foreign-

[26] David L. Jordan and Benjamin I. Page, "Shaping Foreign Policy Opinions: The Role of TV News," *Journal of Conflict Resolution* 36 (June 1992): 227–41. I argue below that criticism from one set of foreign sources—the NATO allies—does influence elite commentators on U.S. foreign policy, if not the mass public.

[27] Bennett, "Press-State Relations," p. 106.

[28] Todd Gitlin, *The Whole World Is Watching: Mass Media in the Making and Unmaking of the New Left* (Berkeley and Los Angeles: University of California Press, 1980).

policy opinion. In contrast, a set of outside-Washington sources that might influence editorial commentary on U.S. foreign policy is the governments of the NATO allies. As NATO is the cornerstone of U.S. foreign policy—in effect a branch of the American foreign-policy establishment—opposition in NATO to a U.S. action could have a substantial impact on American opinion leaders who would otherwise join in a Washington consensus. If Western European reaction to a U.S. intervention is negative, this might lead American commentators who have access to the *New York Times* opinion pages and the *MacNeil/Lehrer Newshour* to question U.S. policy themselves.

As there is just one case in this study (the Gulf War) where one finds significant mass demonstrations against U.S. intervention, and just one case (Libya) where a bipartisan consensus in Washington supported an intervention the NATO allies opposed, a systematic test of these amendments to the indexing hypothesis is not possible. The evidence reported in chapter 5, however, suggests that mass demonstrations (in the *New York Times* news section and on the evening news) and NATO opposition (on the *New York Times* opinion pages and *MacNeil/Lehrer*) are factors that can cause departures from the indexing rule. Neither departure, however, is a major one, if reports on mass demonstrations are framed in negative terms, and if the reaction of the NATO allies is simply an extension of the definition of official debate.

Television News and the Washington Agenda

The case that is most often cited as evidence of the impact of the media—more precisely, television—on U.S. foreign policy is the decision to send American troops to Somalia. Is the case of television news and U.S. intervention in Somalia in 1992, although not examined in the content analysis (which does include the October 1993 phase of that intervention), an exception to the indexing rule? If it is true that television put the crisis in Somalia on the Washington agenda, reported it out of proportion to its position on that agenda, or introduced into public debate the idea that Somalia constituted a crisis the U.S. could do something about, the independent impact of the media on U.S. foreign policy might be greater than the indexing hypothesis predicts.

Does television news sometimes put great pressure on the White House to use military force? To investigate this question, chapter 6 juxtaposes television news stories on Somalia in 1992 and attention to Somalia in Washington. If the independent media hypothesis is correct, the evidence should indicate that television broadcast the crisis in Somalia to Americans before it had emerged as an issue in Washington. A second possibility, one that is consistent with the indexing hypothesis, is that Somalia emerged as an issue in Washington first, before it had received substantial coverage on American television. I pose the same question about the impact of the media in getting the war in Bosnia onto the U.S. foreign-policy agenda in 1992, and in generating an American response to the suppression of the Kurdish rebellion in northern Iraq at the end of the Gulf War in 1991.

I focus on television in examining these three cases because those who argue that the media influenced U.S. policy focus on it. The claim is that television coverage of war and human suffering, with its powerful emotional impact, forced the White House to act; such power has not been attributed to stories on Somalia, Bosnia, and the Iraqi Kurds in the *New York Times*.

Organization

Chapter 2 explains why journalists might be expected to index debate in the news to debate in Washington, examines previous efforts to defend and critique such journalism, and presents the theoretical argument of the book. Chapter 3 examines coverage of U.S. intervention in Grenada and Panama, a juxtaposition that illuminates the issues outlined here and in chapter 2. The focus of chapter 4 is on the August and November phases of the buildup to the Gulf War, also an instructive contrast. Chapter 5 summarizes the findings of the content analysis and investigates a few figures in the Libya, Gulf War (January), and Somalia cases that do not match the general pattern. Chapter 6 examines the influence of television news on the decision to send U.S. troops to Somalia in 1992 and in the cases of Bosnia and the Iraqi Kurds. Chapter 7 evaluates the impact of the news media on U.S. foreign policy and offers some prescriptions for independent journalism.

Two

The Spectrum of Debate in the News

WHY MIGHT one expect American journalists to index the spectrum of debate in the news to the spectrum of debate in Washington? The indexing hypothesis builds on the work of Herbert J. Gans, Gaye Tuchman, Mark Fishman, Leon V. Sigal, and others who observed the operation of news organizations and the construction of news stories.[1] The interpretation of American journalism that emerges in these studies focuses on the powerful set of incentives—pertaining to the need to conserve time, money, and credibility—that encourage reporters to base their stories on the statements of official sources.

Sources of News

It is no mystery why journalists use government officials as news sources. Official sources are the perfect solution to the basic problem journalists confront. Each day, on deadline, journalists have to decide what constitutes news. The world being a vast and complicated place, this is a major task, and rules of thumb are needed.

Although news can happen anywhere, practical considerations limit where reporters are able to look for it. In Sigal's formulation, "To satisfy the requirements of turning out a daily newspaper on deadline with a limited budget and staff, editors have to assign reporters to places where newsworthy information is made public every day. Reporters need sources who can provide information on a regular and timely basis; they are not free to roam or probe at will."[2] A concentration of "places where newsworthy information is made public every day" is found in Washington. The White House, the cabinet departments, Congress, and other offices and agencies of the U.S. government generate an unending flow of statements, briefings, speeches, hearings, resolutions, and other forms of communica-

---

[1] Herbert J. Gans, *Deciding What's News* (New York: Vintage Books, 1980); Mark Fishman, *Manufacturing the News* (Austin: University of Texas Press, 1980); Tuchman, "Objectivity as Strategic Ritual"; Leon V. Sigal, *Reporters and Officials* (Lexington, Mass.: D. C. Heath, 1973).

[2] Leon V. Sigal, "Sources Make the News," in *Reading the News*, ed. Robert Karl Manoff and Michael Schudson (New York: Pantheon Books, 1986), p. 16.

tion on a wide variety of events. In the area of foreign policy, the contrast between the international scale and scope of the U.S. government and the far more modest resources of even the biggest news organizations makes the government an especially attractive source.

Fishman cites "the principle of bureaucratic affinity" to explain why news organizations gravitate toward official sources: "only other bureaucracies can satisfy the input needs of a news bureaucracy."[3] Government agencies—bureaucracies in the modern era—organize their public-relations activities in a manner that is designed to meet the structural requirements of news production, and journalists take full advantage of the services the government offers.[4] As Hallin explains the interaction of journalists and government officials, "The government is organized to provide a timely flow of information, geared to the demands of daily journalism; it is extremely efficient for news organizations to locate their personnel at the channels provided by government."[5] Journalists need sources that are inexpensive and easy to access, precisely what the government provides. Official sources are sometimes evasive on matters of interest to reporters, but enough information is generally dispensed, on or off the record, to constitute a story. This information is not always accurate or illuminating, of course, but it has the great virtue of being inexpensive and easy to obtain.

It is, moreover, presumed to be credible. Journalists who report information that turns out to be inaccurate based on nonofficial sources can be held responsible for the error.[6] The news organization might even be subject to legal action.[7] A journalist who reports information from an official source, however, is not seen as responsible if the information proves to be inaccurate. Instead, the government is blamed for misleading the press. Government officials, although not always credible in the sense that they are believed to be telling the truth, are credible in that it is seen as reasonable for journalists to report what they say.

[3] Fishman, *Manufacturing the News*, p. 143.

[4] On the efforts of the Reagan White House to feed stories to the news media, see Mark Hertsgaard, *On Bended Knee: The Press and the Reagan Presidency* (New York: Farrar, Straus and Giroux, 1988).

[5] Hallin, *The "Uncensored War,"* p. 71.

[6] For an example of what can happen when a journalist uses nonofficial sources who contradict official ones, even when it has *not* been established that the information reported is inaccurate, see Hertsgaard on the troubles Raymond Bonner of the *New York Times* encountered when he reported evidence of a government-sponsored massacre in El Salvador in 1982—just as the White House declared that El Salvador had made "a concerted and significant effort to comply with internationally recognized human rights" (quoted in Hertsgaard, *On Bended Knee*, p. 188)—on the basis of interviews with peasants. Hertsgaard, *On Bended Knee*, pp. 186–91, 196–203.

[7] Tuchman, "Objectivity as Strategic Ritual."

One might have expected to find a trade-off between the goals of minimizing the expenditure of time and money and of maximizing credibility: the faster and cheaper the story, the less credible the story would be. But it turns out that a single set of sources minimizes the expenditure of time and money *and* maximizes presumed credibility. The use of government sources, then, is not just a good solution to the practical needs of news organizations, but an ideal one.

Debating the Indexing Rule

The claim of the indexing hypothesis is that the reliance of journalists on official sources is great enough to cause the spectrum of debate in the news to mirror the spectrum of debate in Washington. This would mean that critical perspectives on government policy that have not been expressed inside the government are ignored or marginalized in the news. Before examining the evidence, however, it is important to establish what is at stake.

Some argue that it is perfectly reasonable for elected officials to set the terms and boundaries of foreign-policy debate in the news, and that the job of the media is to report those issues and alternatives politicians decide to address. In Bennett's formulation of the defense of indexing,

> Governmental definitions of reality are supposed to be, after all, the best approximation of that bedrock of political reality, responsible public opinion. If for some reason the voices of government are unrepresentative or irresponsible, does the responsibility to correct the problem lie with journalists or with the people who elect governments in the first place? Should not responsible journalists report primarily what governments say and let the people form their own reactions?[8]

A democratically elected government, in this view, is "entitled to some margin of discretion in deciding the public interest."[9] If citizens are unhappy with government policy or the terms of debate over it, the logic goes, they can elect new representatives.

For John Zaller, the margin of discretion a democratic government deserves is extensive. Zaller outlines a normative model in which the role of the media is "to convey the policy recommendations of leading political figures, and to indicate, after the dust has settled, whether the advice succeeded or failed."[10] In Zaller's view, citizens operate in practice by de-

---

[8] Bennett, " Press-State Relations," p. 109.

[9] Ibid., p. 105. Bennett is critical of indexing under certain conditions (see below).

[10] John Zaller, "Elite Leadership of Mass Opinion: New Evidence from the Gulf War," in Bennett and Paletz, *Taken by Storm*, p. 202.

termining the policy positions of political leaders they respect and adopt-
ing those positions as their own, unless there is clear evidence that a policy
is not working as designed. In this minimalist version of citizenship, voters
are simply expected to figure out what policies their favorite political
leaders support, and to note in due course their success or failure. If a
policy is determined to have failed, voters then have the option of punish-
ing those responsible for it. To enable the public to achieve this standard
of citizenship, journalists need simply to document the words and deeds
of elected officials and report policy outcomes; critical analysis of policy
decisions is not required. For Zaller, then, the execution/outcome angle
described in chapter 1 is enough to enable citizens to fulfill their democratic duties.

For David L. Paletz, too, it is unreasonable to expect journalists to expand the spectrum of foreign-policy debate in the news beyond the debate
found in Washington. Paletz suggests that "ascribing the purpose of reporting as enabling and supporting informed public debate about policy
questions through representing (and evaluating) the range of policy alternatives worth considering in such a debate places an untoward, even un-
achievable expectation on the news media."[11] The role of the media, Paletz
argues, is simply to "report the news," not to offer critical analysis of policy
decisions.[12]

The argument most often made in response to defenders of indexing is
that it is the responsibility of the press to stimulate public debate and to
maximize the diversity of perspectives in the news. In a study of newspaper coverage of the early stages of the buildup to the Gulf War, Dorman
and Livingston question whether "information reported by the news
media encouraged or undermined vigorous democratic debate" and conclude that "the news media fell short of helping to create a robust culture
of debate."[13] Entman and Page suggest that reporters covering the
buildup in the Gulf could have "defined their roles more self-consciously
as stimulators of public participation and debate," featuring "opposition
voices, no matter what their institutional roles or power."[14] For these authors, reporting critical perspectives on foreign-policy decisions is seen as
a fundamental role of journalism, contrary to the position of Zaller and
Paletz.

[11] David L. Paletz, "Just Deserts?" in Bennett and Paletz, *Taken by Storm,* pp. 285–86.
[12] Ibid., p. 280.
[13] William A. Dorman and Steven Livingston, "News and Historical Content: The Establishing Phase of the Persian Gulf Policy Debate," in Bennett and Paletz, *Taken by Storm,* pp.
64, 76.
[14] Robert M. Entman and Benjamin I. Page, "The News before the Storm: The Iraq War
Debate and the Limits to Media Independence," in Bennett and Paletz, *Taken by Storm,*
p. 97.

In a somewhat more systematic formulation of this argument, Herbert J. Gans argues for "multiperspectivism" in the media, on the ground that news dominated by political (and economic) elites reinforces the position of the powerful and organized in society. Instead, journalists should report the news "in terms of all known perspectives." For Gans, the news "must enable all sectors of nation and society to place their actions and activities—and messages—in the symbolic arena."[15]

Cass Sunstein offers a variation on Gans's theme, writing that the American constitutional regime is "designed to have an important deliberative feature."[16] In this deliberative democracy, institutional and social position should not be a factor in deciding who gets access to public debate. Instead, Sunstein declares, "arguments are to count if good reasons are offered on their behalf."[17] Sunstein concludes that journalists should consult a diverse spectrum of sources on the basis of "a norm of political equality, in which arguments matter but power and authority do not."[18]

What neither Gans nor Sunstein explains, in practical terms that might be of use to journalists, is *what* alternative viewpoints should be reported. "What counts as appropriate diversity," Sunstein notes, "is of course controversial." But his contribution on this point is simply a definition of diversity: "I suggest only that a broad spectrum of opinion must be represented, that people must be allowed to hear sharply divergent views, and that it is important to find not merely the conventional wisdom and the reasons that can be offered on its behalf, but also challenges to the conventional wisdom from a variety of different perspectives."[19] Increased diversity may be a good idea, but beyond this general principle Gans and Sunstein offer no practical guidelines that journalists might use in deciding what perspectives should get more coverage.[20] Nor do these authors offer much of a response to the charge that increasing the spectrum of viewpoints in the news would simply enable marginal and extreme figures to undermine the efforts of elected officials and political parties to structure public debate.[21]

---

[15] Gans, *Deciding What's News,* p. 312.

[16] Cass R. Sunstein, *Democracy and the Problem of Free Speech* (New York: Free Press, 1993), p. 19.

[17] Ibid., p. 20.

[18] Ibid., p. 19.

[19] Ibid., pp. 21–22.

[20] Gans does offer some general ideas about where to find alternative viewpoints—focus more on the nation and less on the government, and explore the perspective of ordinary people—that point in the direction of the argument of this book (*Deciding What's News,* p. 313).

[21] Sunstein does offer an unconventional constitutional interpretation under which journalists must maximize the diversity of perspectives in the news. He argues that the First Amendment enshrines a positive right of citizen access to the public sphere and is offended

The premise behind the Gans-Sunstein position is that certain interests are underrepresented in government in a capitalist democracy and therefore need other avenues of access to the news. But what those interests are is a politically contested question. Liberals argue, for example, that the poor are underrepresented in a political system that business interests dominate. Conservatives, however, claim that business interests are underrepresented in a government that pays too much attention to the needs of the poor. Arguments that specific interests are underrepresented in Washington are therefore problematic as a prescription for journalists. In response to criticism from one side of the political spectrum, journalists can respond that they are hearing just the opposite argument from the other side, and conclude that they must be getting it about right.

Bennett's critique of indexing encounters the same problem. Bennett argues that departures from indexing are justified "as checks against unrepresentative or otherwise irresponsible governments."[22] But the example he offers of an "irresponsible" government—the Reagan administration in its 1986 campaign to brand Democratic opponents of Contra aid as "soft on Communism"[23]—demonstrates the weakness of the argument. For while liberals believed Reagan's tactics to be an extraordinary case of red-baiting, conservatives claimed that Reagan had simply offered a sound critique of the Democratic position. The problem is that "irresponsible" government is hard to define in terms that liberals and conservatives do not dispute. This undermines the effort to construct a general critique of indexing, as Bennett's argument is bound to strike journalists as resting on a liberal political agenda, the ideological opposite of conservative arguments that the news was biased *against* Contra aid.[24] Bennett's critique of indexing is therefore not going to convince journalists to change their coverage.[25] But in pointing out that "political

---

if journalists do not report a diverse spectrum of debate (see Sunstein, *Democracy and Free Speech,* chap. 2). My own argument is also based on an interpretation of the First Amendment, but one that is consistent with the prevailing liberal interpretation, not a controversial departure such as Sunstein proposes.

[22] Bennett, "Press-State Relations," p. 104.

[23] Ibid., p. 113.

[24] For an argument that the American media reported the Nicaraguan revolution from a pro-Sandinista perspective, see Joshua Muravchik, *News Coverage of the Sandinista Revolution* (Washington, D.C.: American Enterprise Institute for Public Policy Research, 1988). See also Shirley Christian, "Covering the Sandinistas: The Foregone Conclusions of the Fourth Estate," in *Reporters under Fire: U.S. Media Coverage of Conflicts in Lebanon and Central America,* ed. Landrum R. Bolling (Boulder, Colo.: Westview Press, 1985), pp. 119–37.

[25] Bennett also argues that a divergence of government policy and public opinion is ground for reporting critical perspectives ("Press-State Relations," p. 104). But the requirement that critical public opinion exist *before* sources outside of the government are consulted

conditions" can lead critics of U.S. foreign policy in Washington to fall silent, Bennett breaks the ground on which the argument of this book is constructed.[26]

The Watchdog and the Mirror

The argument that journalists should report a diverse mix of perspectives on U.S. foreign policy must ultimately confront an ambiguity at the heart of American journalism, where two contradictory ideals coexist. In Hallin's formulation, under the *watchdog ideal* journalists are expected to investigate and expose unsound government policies and misleading official statements, acting as "champions of truth and openness, checking the tendency of the powerful to conceal and dissemble."[27] One media and politics textbook writes that the watchdog ideal demands that the press function as "a beacon of responsibility shining a light on wrongdoing, making sure that government does not exceed its bounds and exposing the truth."[28] In the process of pursuing the watchdog ideal, journalists are expected to introduce new perspectives into the public sphere and stimulate public debate.

The indexing rule is in clear violation of the watchdog ideal, as it is hard for the press to perform the watchdog function if politicians are granted the power to set the terms and boundaries of debate in the news. The analogy would be to a watchdog that consulted members of the intruding party as to whether it was appropriate to bark—not a very useful animal. The watchdog ideal might therefore seem to offer a powerful critique of the indexing rule, as it establishes a standard of responsible journalism that news indexed to debate in Washington cannot achieve.

In pursuing the watchdog ideal, however, journalists clash with the *mirror ideal*, which tells them (in Paletz's phrase) simply to "report the news," free of interpretation and analysis. Doris A. Graber writes that under the mirror ideal journalists aim to "observe the world around them and report what they see as accurately and objectively as possible. . . . They reflect whatever comes to their attention; they do not shape it in any way."[29] Edward Jay Epstein explains the mirror ideal in similar terms: "A mirror

---

means this is a narrow exception to the indexing rule. If U.S. foreign policy has bipartisan support in Washington, the public might not be exposed to information and analysis that could inspire critical opinion in the first place (more on this below).

[26] Ibid., p. 113.

[27] Hallin, *The "Uncensored War,"* p. 5.

[28] Stephen Ansolabehere, Roy Behr, and Shanto Iyengar, *The Media Game: American Politics in the Television Age* (New York: Macmillan, 1993), p. 221.

[29] Graber, *Mass Media and Politics,* p. 76.

makes no decisions, it simply reflects what occurs in front of it."[30] A mirror does not champion truth and openness or shine a light on wrongdoing, unless of course wrongdoing happens to materialize before it.

Epstein points out that the mirror ideal cannot be achieved in practice: "What is reflected on television as national news depends, unlike a 'mirror,' on certain predecisions about where camera crews and correspondents will be assigned."[31] As time in the newscast and space on the page are limited, decisions must be made to reflect some aspects of reality in the journalistic mirror and not to reflect others. But despite the inevitable barriers to its realization, the mirror ideal has great metaphorical power as a goal toward which journalists aspire, as it resonates with commonsense notions of accurate, objective reporting and shields journalists against charges that their stories have undue influence on the political process.

As the watchdog and mirror ideals coexist at the heart of American journalism, an appeal to one is easy to counter with an appeal to the other. Journalists charged under the watchdog ideal with failing to report critical perspectives on government policies can offer the mirror ideal in their defense, as evidence that critical analysis of government policies is not in their job description. Indeed, the mirror ideal is a meritorious counterweight to the adversarial watchdog ideal; without the mirror ideal as a balance, journalism geared toward the watchdog ideal could make it hard for politicians to govern.[32] The strongest critique of indexing, therefore, is one that is consistent with the watchdog *and* mirror ideals. Such a critique is possible once the connection between "reporting the news" (central to the mirror ideal) and reporting perspectives outside the spectrum of Washington debate (central to the watchdog ideal) is established.

The Press and the Logic of Politics

The critique of indexing in this book does not rest on the proposition that journalists should maximize the spectrum of viewpoints in the news or stimulate public debate. Nor is it based on a politically contested interpretation of what interests are underrepresented in American politics. Building on Bennett's observation about the impact of "electoral incentives" on the spectrum of debate in Washington,[33] the argument is based instead on an inevitable aspect of democratic politics that has profound implica-

---

[30] Edward Jay Epstein, *News from Nowhere: Television and the News* (New York: Random House, 1973), p. 16.

[31] Ibid.

[32] Patterson, *Out of Order.*

[33] Bennett, "Press-State Relations," p. 106.

tions for efforts to realize in practice the First Amendment ideal of a press independent of government.

At the heart of democratic politics, E. E. Schattschneider argues in *The Semisovereign People,* is a process of agenda setting, in which some issues are placed on the agenda of government and others are marginalized or ignored. Out of the universe of potential issues, just a fraction emerge as the focus of conflict in Washington. "Americans hold more elections than all the rest of the world put together," Schattschneider observes, "but there must be millions of issues on which we cannot vote."[34] This paradox is explained as follows:

> There are billions of potential conflicts in any modern society, but *only a few become significant.* The reduction of the number of conflicts is an essential part of politics. Politics deals with the domination and subordination of conflicts.[35]

As politicians and parties form strategic coalitions designed to win elections, certain issues emerge as the focus of conflict in Washington, while others are marginalized or ignored.

The narrowing of the focus of conflict is not simply a function of objective conditions to which politicians and parties respond. Political scientists have found that strategic political calculations, sometimes independent of judgments on the substantive merits of issues and alternatives, are a major determinant of the positions that politicians and parties stake out and defend.[36] The response of the opposition party to a White House action must therefore be understood as a strategic decision. Although other factors influence the behavior of politicians,[37] strategic political calculations structure the set of issues and alternatives politicians and parties decide to address. In the process, "Some issues are organized into politics while others are organized out."[38]

Strategic politicians are attuned to certain social realities, of course, and are very interested in the preferences of voters. But a given set of social realities and public preferences could produce various alignments of political parties, depending on the strategies the parties use and the conflicts they decide to exploit. The connection between prevailing social realities and public preferences, and the positioning of the parties across the spec-

---

[34] E. E. Schattschneider, *The Semisovereign People: A Realist's View of Democracy in America* (New York: Holt, Rinehart and Winston, 1960), p. 71.

[35] Ibid., p. 66, emphasis in original.

[36] See, for example, David R. Mayhew, *Congress: The Electoral Connection* (New Haven, Conn.: Yale University Press, 1974); and William H. Riker, *The Art of Political Manipulation* (New Haven, Conn.: Yale University Press, 1986).

[37] On the multiple goals of politicians, see Richard F. Fenno, *Home Style: House Members in Their Districts* (Boston: Little, Brown, 1978).

[38] Schattschneider, *The Semisovereign People,* p. 71.

trum of potential issues, Schattschneider argues, is indeterminate. The spectrum of debate in Washington is just one possible representation of public preferences and the public interest. This general phenomenon is well established in political science, but its implications for the question of press-state relations have gone unexamined.

Schattschneider argues that too much is made of open conflict in Washington, as opposed to how politics sets the Washington agenda in the first place: "we have looked for the wrong kind of conflict (conflict *within* the government) and have underestimated the extent to which *the government itself as a whole* has been in conflict with other power systems."[39] To focus on "conflict *within* the government" is to render invisible the decisions that set the Washington agenda, decisions that determine what issues and alternatives are going to be the focus of political conflict inside the government. For Schattschneider, *"the definition of the alternatives is the supreme instrument of power."* This is because "the definition of the alternatives is the choice of conflicts, and the choice of conflicts allocates power."[40]

Governments, of course, require agendas in order to govern, and democratic politics is a system for establishing agendas. Schattschneider argues that "Any political system which attempted to exploit all of the tensions in the community would be blown to bits."[41] In Patterson's formulation, "To criticize politicians for 'playing politics' is to fault a process that is necessary to reconcile society's competing interests."[42] But while politicians must act strategically if democracy is to function, must the media report the news from inside the boundaries strategic politicians set? If politicians focus on some issues and alternatives and ignore others for strategic reasons, then for journalists to use the spectrum of issues and alternatives generated in Washington to set the terms and boundaries of debate in the news is to reproduce and reinforce in the news the strategic calculations of politicians.

To report the news from a vantage point independent of government, journalists need to be independent of the politics that determines what the conflict inside the government is about in the first place. But the indexing rule precludes this. News that is indexed to debate in Washington offers critical analysis of Democrats from the viewpoint of Republicans, and Republicans from the viewpoint of Democrats, but ignores perspectives that have simply been "organized out" of American politics in the strategic decisions of politicians. Contrary to the claim that this form of journalism just "reports the news," indexing reports the news *from the*

---

[39] Ibid., p. 126, emphasis in original.
[40] Ibid., p. 68, emphasis in original.
[41] Ibid., p. 66.
[42] Patterson, *Out of Order*, p. 241.

vantage point of strategic politicians, debating issues politicians are debating and ignoring issues politicians are ignoring. Not just the watchdog ideal, then, but also the mirror ideal is violated under the indexing rule, for what the mirror reflects is not an objective version of *what happened,* but the spectrum of interpretations of what happened that politics has produced.

Journalists who report the news inside the terms of Washington debate are independent of government in a formal, legal sense but have in effect turned over to official actors the power to set the news agenda and the spectrum of debate in the news. If politicians are in consensus, the indexing rule reproduces and reinforces their consensus; the press does not offer critical analysis of government policies unless actors inside the government have done so first. It is this aspect of indexing that violates the First Amendment ideal of a press independent of government.

My argument is *not* that journalists should adjust their foreign-policy coverage to focus more attention on explicating the strategic calculations that structure Washington debate. As Patterson and others have demonstrated, media coverage of elections and domestic-policy debates overflows with stories about the strategic aspect of American politics, and there is reason to believe this has contributed to the political cynicism of the American public.[43] Cappella and Jamieson write that "strategic news frames" suggest to voters that "the motives [of politicians] are self-interested . . .—manipulative, dishonest, self-centered, deceitful, pandering," and therefore encourage a cynical response.[44] Although I have argued that democratic politics *is* at heart a strategic contest for power, I do not believe the press should encourage citizens to experience politics in these terms.

Foreign-policy news that focused on explicating the strategic calculations of politicians would not (as a rule) misrepresent their motives and would in fact be a solution to the problem of the news reproducing and reinforcing strategic calculations made inside the government. But it would come at the cost of increasing the political cynicism of a jaded and disengaged public, which might just decide to tune out foreign-policy debate if it were framed in strategic terms. A better solution would be for journalists simply to stop letting the spectrum of debate in Washington determine the spectrum of debate in the news. For this to happen, journalists need to consult sources who are not players in the political game, whose views are not shaped by its incentives, and who are free to address issues and alternatives that politicians have decided to ignore.

[43] Patterson, *Out of Order.*
[44] Joseph N. Cappella and Kathleen Hall Jamieson, *Spiral of Cynicism: The Press and the Public Good* (New York: Oxford University Press, 1997), pp. 166–67.

Experts and the Public

The sources journalists consult on U.S. foreign policy include players, experts, and the public.[45] Players are politicians and government officials. Experts (for the most part) are former politicians and government officials, persons affiliated with Washington think tanks, and university academics. The public is the mass public and those citizens who manifest a real interest and engagement in foreign policy. Under the indexing rule, journalists consult players, Washington experts, and mass opinion data in their coverage of U.S. interventions. To increase their independence, journalists could consult players, experts inside *and outside* of Washington, and mass opinion data *and citizens with a real interest and engagement in foreign policy.* To be more independent of government, in other words, journalists need to expand their operating definitions of foreign-policy experts and public opinion.

On domestic issues, interest groups are used as news sources and are often critical of government policies. On the health care issue, for example, interested parties include doctors, hospitals, senior citizens, insurance companies, drug manufacturers, employers, and others. When health care is on the Washington agenda, representatives of these interests appear in the news.

Organizations representing interested parties have not, however, been major contributors to public debate on military intervention. A leading textbook on U.S. foreign policy concludes that "interest groups exert a far greater impact on domestic than on foreign policy issues."[46] Interest groups are most influential on foreign policy "when the issue is not in the public spotlight, attended by the mass media,"[47] a condition that does not describe military intervention. A number of public-interest organizations focus on foreign policy and offer reaction to military interventions, but such organizations do not often get access to the news (see below).

One powerful interest that has a major stake in U.S. foreign policy and does have access to the news is business. But business, as a rule, has found U.S. foreign policy to be quite consistent with its interests. In the Cold War, Washington supported anti-Communists against Communists—real and imagined—the anti-Communists being the side more interested in economic engagement with the United States on terms favorable to American business. In the post–Cold War era, a major organizing principle of U.S. foreign policy has been to secure investment opportunities, market

---

[45] Chapter 1 explains why foreign sources are excluded from the analysis.

[46] Charles W. Kegley Jr., and Eugene R. Wittkopf, *American Foreign Policy: Pattern and Process* (New York: St. Martin's Press, 1987), p. 278.

[47] Ibid., p. 279.

access, and oil for American business. The objectives of U.S. foreign policy therefore continue to match the interests of American business. On some aspects of foreign economic policy business is divided, but there has not been a military intervention in the post-Vietnam era in which such a division has materialized.

Finding no great clash of interested parties in the United States, journalists turn to experts to describe and explain U.S. intervention. But do the experts consulted represent the balance of American expert opinion? Zaller argues that "if there is a significant fraction of mainstream expert opinion that holds a particular view, the press will look for ways to use that view as the basis of news reports."[48] Zaller does point to possible "bias in recruitment to the expert communities," and expresses concern that "professional incentive structures" could introduce distortions into the analysis expert communities produce,[49] but he does not seem to view these problems as major ones. Contrary to Zaller's confidence that media coverage of expert opinion is balanced, my evidence shows that journalists turn disproportionately to certain sectors of the foreign-policy expert community that are *not* representative of the balance of expert opinion: present and former politicians and government officials, and Washington think tanks.

Although not active players in the political game, former government officials and Washington think tank experts have incentives and inclinations to express views consistent with those being expressed inside the government. Former government officials are often future government officials, interested in not alienating those who might elect or appoint them to office. Such experts have also been steeped in a pragmatic policymaking culture that rejects alternatives that go beyond what is seen as politically possible.[50] While exceptions exist, most former government officials express views that fall inside the boundaries of Democratic-Republican debate.

The objective of the Washington think tank, James A. Smith observes, is to "define the middle ground and provid[e] an environment in which the knowledge of experts can be channeled to serve political ends."[51] If think tank experts (or former government officials—the sets often overlap)

---

[48] John R. Zaller, *The Nature and Origins of Mass Opinion* (Cambridge: Cambridge University Press, 1992), p. 316.

[49] Ibid., p. 325.

[50] See Alexander L. George, *Bridging the Gap: Theory and Practice in Foreign Policy* (Washington, D.C.: United States Institute of Peace, 1993); and Philip Zelikow, "Foreign Policy Engineering: From Theory to Practice and Back Again," *International Security* 18 (spring 1994): 143–71.

[51] James A. Smith, *The Idea Brokers: Think Tanks and the Rise of the New Policy Elite* (New York: Free Press, 1991), p. 213.

hope to get the attention of policymakers, their proposals must be seen as
politically viable. For this reason, think tank experts—especially on foreign policy—do not often express opinions that clash with the Washington
agenda. Washington think tanks cannot therefore be expected to counter
the indexing effect. For this journalists must turn to sources outside of
Washington.

The best place to find foreign-policy experts outside of Washington is
the university. University experts, as a rule, are engaged in a different activity than those operating in or near policymaking circles. In George's view:
"Academics aim at increasing general knowledge and wisdom about international relations; practitioners are more interested in the type of knowledge that increases their ability to influence and control the course of
events." This is an important distinction, for "In the role of policymaker,
individuals . . . need uncomplicated diagnoses and solutions in order to
take action."[52] Unfettered by the need for analysis to prescribe politically
viable action, academics are free to address issues and alternatives that
experts tied to Washington decline to explore.

Timothy Garton Ash has argued that academics (or "intellectuals") and
politicians

> have, and should have, a different role, which is reflected, crucially, in a different
> use of language. If a politician gives a partial, one-sided, indeed self-censored
> account of a particular issue, he is simply doing his job. And if he manages to
> "sell" the part as the whole then he is doing his job effectively.
>
> If an intellectual does that, he is not doing his job; he has failed in it.[53]

The argument is not that the academic is "the guardian or high priest of
. . . Truth with a capital T,"[54] but that the job description of the academic
differs in a fundamental way from that of the politician or Washington
insider. The job of the academic is to observe and comment on events
from a vantage point independent of government and politics. The job of
the politician is to engage effectively in government and politics. Politicians who do not choose their words cautiously, with an eye to political
incentives and constraints, simply are not doing their job.

To make this distinction is not to criticize politicians, but to observe
that politicians and academics play different social roles and consequently
say different things. For Garton Ash,

> there is a necessary and healthy division of labor in a liberal state between inde-
> pendent intellectuals and professional politicians. Arguably this is as important-

[52] George, *Bridging the Gap*, p. 9.

[53] Timothy Garton Ash, "Prague: Intellectuals and Politicians," *New York Review of Books*,
January 12, 1995, pp. 35–36.

[54] Ibid., p. 36.

TABLE 2.1

Affiliations of Guests on *MacNeil/Lehrer Newshour*
(Eight Military Interventions)

	Number	*Percent*
Former government official	84	31
Journalist	57	21
United States government	55	20
Foreign	30	11
Washington think tank	12	4
Ordinary person / participant	10	4
University academic	8	3
Business	8	3
Other	5	2
Public-interest organization	2	1
Total	271	

Note: Guests who are former government officials *and* have university appointments or think-tank affiliations are counted as former government officials.

as the formal separation of powers between executive, legislature, and judiciary. It is part of the larger and all-important creative tension between the state and civil society.[55]

It is important to note that the commentary of academics need not differ in *form* from that of politicians. The virtue Garton Ash sees in academic analysis is not abstraction or complexity, but independence of the state, something those operating in or near government do not have.

On a continuum from Washington insiders to independent outsiders— or in Garton Ash's terms, from "state" to "society"—former government officials and Washington think tank experts fall much closer to the insider/ state end, their claim to expertise resting on experience in or near government. Yet as table 2.1 indicates, out of 271 guests who on the *MacNeil/Lehrer Newshour* discussed the military interventions examined in this study, 35 percent were former government officials or Washington think tank experts; just 3 percent were university academics.

As *MacNeil/Lehrer* is noted for the diversity of its sources, the disparity should be even greater in other news media. Space clearly exists, then, for journalists to consult more foreign-policy experts outside of Washington.

Because of the inside/outside Washington bifurcation of the foreign-policy expert community, one must question Zaller's decision to locate

[55] Ibid., p. 35.

"the real responsibility for selecting the ideas that reach the public with the press's sources."[56] If one segment of the foreign-policy expert community is featured in the news and the other is marginalized, the problem lies not in how expert knowledge is produced, but in how journalists select experts to appear in the news.

Just as the media's definition of experts could be expanded, so could their definition of public opinion. Although journalists often report mass opinion data and conduct person-on-the-street interviews to illustrate the poll findings, this method of gauging the views of the public is problematic. If people get their information about foreign policy from the news, and the news is indexed to Washington debate, then aggregate public opinion is not independent of Washington debate, but to a great extent a function of it. Polls finding public support for a policy that has bipartisan support in Washington therefore have a circular quality.[57] It is hard then to justify the use of mass opinion data showing support for U.S. foreign policy as grounds for marginalizing critical perspectives in the news, if critics of the policy have not had a chance to explain their position to the public.

Although "poll results and public opinion are terms that are used almost synonymously" in the modern era, Benjamin Ginsberg observes that the mass opinion poll is just one measure of public opinion, one in which citizens play a passive role.[58] A second measure is the reaction of interested, engaged citizens. The virtue of the poll is that it compensates for the fact that engaged citizens are not representative of the mass public. The virtue of the engaged citizen, however, is that polls tend to "submerge individuals with strongly held views in a more apathetic mass public."[59] For example, Ginsberg argues that when the Nixon administration used polls showing a "silent majority" (if not an interested or engaged one) supporting the Vietnam War to justify ignoring the demands of the antiwar movement, "the polls came to be used against those persons who truly had opinions."[60] The point is not that one measure of public opinion is better than the other, but that journalists could report polling data *and* the reaction of those citizens most interested and engaged on foreign-policy issues. Such people vanish into the inert masses in aggregate polling data

[56] Zaller, *Nature and Origins,* p. 319.

[57] On the impact of Washington debate on public opinion, see Brody, *Assessing the President;* and Zaller, *Nature and Origins.*

[58] Benjamin Ginsberg, "How Polling Transforms Public Opinion," in *Manipulating Public Opinion: Essays on Public Opinion as a Dependent Variable,* ed. Michael Margolis and Gary A. Mauser (Pacific Grove, Calif.: Brooks/Cole, 1989), p. 273.

[59] Ginsberg, "Polling Transforms Public Opinion," p. 276.

[60] Ibid., p. 277.

but are much less inclined than the mass public simply to mirror opinions that have been expressed in Washington debate.

When Zaller writes that people who are more informed about politics are *more* likely to echo opinions articulated in Washington, he is distinguishing between *relatively* more and less informed members of the mass public.[61] But as researchers have demonstrated, "On most issues, the great majority of citizens are inattentive and uninformed."[62] My focus here is on the small percentage of the public that is *most* attentive and informed about foreign policy, those who are in some way mobilized to influence it. As this set of citizens constitutes less than 5 percent of the public even on domestic issues[63]—and on foreign policy the figure could be well below 5 percent—it barely registers in mass opinion polls.[64] Neuman observes that mass opinion data offer mere "hints and fragments of evidence about this activist elite," a "very small, attentive top stratum of the mass public."[65] It is the *most* interested and engaged citizens—not a significant factor in the aggregate polling data Zaller uses—who might be expected to offer educated commentary on U.S. foreign policy that is independent of Washington debate.[66]

Public-interest organizations that focus on foreign policy offer a window on the reaction of engaged citizens to military interventions. Eleven national peace organizations with over 25 local branches were active in the 1980s,[67] as were hundreds of civic, professional, scientific, and religious organizations around the nation with an interest in foreign policy.[68] Their numbers experienced some decline with the end of the Cold War, but such organizations continued to speak out on U.S. foreign policy in the 1990s.

[61] Zaller, *Nature and Origins,* chap. 6.

[62] W. Russell Neuman, *The Paradox of Mass Politics: Knowledge and Opinion in the American Electorate* (Cambridge, Mass: Harvard University Press, 1986), p. 186. See chapter 2 of *Paradox of Mass Politics* for a review of the relevant literature, including a critique of the revisionist claim that the ignorance of the mass public has been overstated.

[63] Ibid, p. 170.

[64] Neuman (ibid., p. 186) writes: "For many political matters the effective size of this group could be much smaller [than 5 percent], measuring a fraction of one percent of the population as a whole."

[65] Ibid, pp. 187, 186.

[66] Neuman writes that "political elites [in the United States] perceive and act within the constraints of an attentive public will" (ibid., p. 186). My argument is that this process does not function as Neuman describes on foreign-policy issues, because of the bifurcated nature of the foreign-policy expert community (inside/outside Washington).

[67] Elise Boulding, "The Early Eighties Peak of the Peace Movement," in *Peace Action in the Eighties: Social Science Perspectives,* ed. Sam Marullo and John Lofland (New Brunswick, N.J.: Rutgers University Press, 1990), p. 23.

[68] Carl Conetta, *Peace Research Book: A Comprehensive Guide to the Issues, Organizations, and Literature, 1988–1989* (Cambridge, Mass: Ballinger, 1988).

Although public-interest organizations that oppose hawkish policies out-number those in support (perhaps because supporters are well represented in the Department of Defense and the Republican Party and see no need to organize on their own), the idea is not that journalists should grant critics of military intervention special access to the news. It is simply that journalists should report manifestations of public opinion that are inde-pendent of Washington debate.

The argument in this chapter about the political logic behind the set-ting of the Washington agenda suggests that the inability of an organiza-tion to win support for its position inside the government is not clear evidence that the position is unsound or justifiably marginalized. In the early 1980s, the positions of major national organizations such as SANE/Freeze and the Committee in Solidarity with the People of El Salvador (CISPES) often matched those of Democrats in Congress. I argue in the next chapter that in the mid-1980s the Democrats made a strategic deci-sion—based on a political calculation, not a reassessment of the merits of hawkish foreign policies or a change in public preferences—to abandon positions that SANE/Freeze and CISPES, not guided by electoral incen-tives, continued to defend.

It is true that members of public-interest organizations constitute a small fraction of the public. Yet if one weighs in the balance the natural barriers those who organize to achieve a public good such as a noninter-ventionist foreign policy have to overcome,[69] the modest size of these orga-nizations as a percentage of the mass public should not be ground for rejecting their claim to space in the public sphere. Coverage of the reaction of those citizens with the greatest concern about foreign policy and mobi-lized to affect it could create a more even balance between the (legitimate) objectives of reporting a representative picture of public opinion, and re-porting public opinion in a form that is independent of Washington de-bate. It is the virtue of independence that public-interest organizations possess. As table 2.1 indicates, however, just 1 percent of the 271 guests on the *MacNeil/Lehrer Newshour* examined in this study represented public-interest organizations.

Letters to the editor offer a second measure of public reaction to U.S. foreign policy that is independent of Washington debate. If, despite posi-tive media coverage, an intervention that wins bipartisan support in Wash-ington generates a substantial volume of critical letters to the editor, this is evidence that support is not as solid or deep outside of Washington as the polls might suggest.

---

[69] Mancur Olson, *The Logic of Collective Action* (Cambridge, Mass.: Harvard University Press, 1971).

As Ginsberg observes, when poll data contradict other measures of public opinion, "it is almost invariably the polls that are presumed to be correct."[70] But it is hard to defend the use of polls as grounds for ignoring the critical views of an engaged minority if the critics have not had a chance to make their case to the public in the first place. If polls are not to "submerge individuals with strongly held views in a more apathetic mass public,"[71] other measures of public opinion, sensitive to citizens who manifest a real interest in foreign policy, not just those offering a "Yes" or "No" on the telephone under the influence of Washington debate, need to be reported.

Independent media coverage, in sum, demands that journalists balance perspectives inside or close to the state with perspectives in American society, interviewing not just Washington insiders but foreign-policy experts outside of Washington, and not just the mass public but interested, engaged citizens. This does not require a dramatic departure from existing journalistic practice. It simply requires that journalists expand their definitions of experts and the public.

[70] Ginsberg, "Polling Transforms Public Opinion," p. 273.
[71] Ibid., p. 276.

Three

Grenada and Panama

THE UNITED STATES invaded Grenada in 1983 and Panama in 1989 on the grounds that forces in those countries had endangered American lives, threatened the United States with Communism (in Grenada) or drug trafficking (in Panama), and refused to practice democracy. Foreign-policy experts and engaged citizens in the United States debated these premises. Had American lives been in real danger? Could other means have been found to protect them? Had the objective of stopping Communism or drug trafficking required a full-scale military intervention? Could unilateral military action, even in the name of democracy, be justified under international law?

Discussion of media coverage of the Grenada and Panama invasions tends to focus on official restrictions on the press.[1] U.S. forces barred journalists from Grenada for three days and obstructed those who tried to get to the island. The Pentagon flew a pool of reporters into Panama but held them on a military base for several hours until the heaviest fighting had ended. These efforts at censorship certainly affected the ability of the media to report what was happening on the ground. But they should not have stopped journalists from gathering information about Grenada and Panama from sources in the United States, and from questioning experts and citizens about the wisdom and justification of U.S. policy.

News coverage of the Grenada invasion, Iyengar and Simon assert, "tended to propagate the worldview and policy preferences of the [Reagan] administration."[2] Bennett describes a continuum from "open information flow" to "closed information flow" and declares that Grenada and Panama "fall toward the closed end of the continuum," where few critical perspectives appear in the news and "there is little ground established for evaluating policies or holding officials accountable."[3] Yet neither Iyengar and Simon nor Bennett offers evidence that the coverage of the

[1] See, for example, John R. MacArthur, *Second Front: Censorship and Propaganda in the Gulf War* (New York: Hill and Wang, 1992).

[2] Shanto Iyengar and Adam Simon, "News Coverage of the Gulf Crisis and Public Opinion: A Study of Agenda-Setting, Priming, and Framing," in Bennett and Paletz, *Taken by Storm*, p. 183.

[3] W. Lance Bennett, "The News about Foreign Policy," in Bennett and Paletz, *Taken by Storm*, p. 21.

⌜Grenada and Panama invasions matches their description. This chapter investigates the spectrum of debate in the news on U.S. intervention in Grenada and Panama, a question others have passed over in favor of the censorship issue. Overt acts of official censorship, it turns out, do not have the decisive impact one might expect: the more heavily censored Grenada operation received much more critical media coverage.

Parallel Interventions

What makes the Grenada-Panama comparison instructive is that the United States offered similar justifications for the two interventions, and those justifications were subject to similar critiques. The justifications focused on the need to protect American lives, fight Communism (in Grenada) or drug trafficking (in Panama), and promote democracy. The critiques focused on the magnitude of the threat Grenada and Panama posed to Americans and to U.S. interests, the need for military intervention to deal with whatever threat existed, and the standing of U.S. action under international law.

The Reagan administration cited the need to "rescue" several hundred Americans at a medical school in Grenada as the primary reason for U.S. intervention. It is clear that the overthrow of Grenadian prime minister Maurice Bishop by a pro-Cuban faction had created what Secretary of State George Schultz described as "a vacuum of governmental authority" and "an atmosphere of violent uncertainty" on the island.[4] It is not clear, however, that the safety of the American students had been jeopardized. One study concludes:

> There is no argument about the American medical students being frightened. Whether or not they were truly in danger was debatable. The chancellor of the medical school . . . at first hotly denied any danger to the students, saying he had been personally assured by the coup leaders that they meant to guarantee the safety of the students. Later, for whatever reason, he changed his mind and agreed, if less than wholeheartedly, that the students may have been in danger.[5]

As for the students themselves, some believed they had been in danger; others believed they had not.[6] Although the White House asserted that the

---

[4] Kai P. Schoenhals and Richard A. Melanson, *Revolution and Intervention in Grenada: The New Jewel Movement, the United States, and the Caribbean* (Boulder, Colo.: Westview Press, 1985), pp. 147–48.

[5] G. F. Illingworth, "Grenada in Retrospect," in *American Intervention in Grenada: The Implication of Operation "Urgent Fury,"* ed. Peter M. Dunn and Bruce W. Watson (Boulder, Colo.: Westview Press, 1985), p. 132.

[6] Robert D. McFadden, "From Rescued Students, Gratitude and Praise," *New York Times,* October 28, 1983, A1.

airport in Grenada had been shut down—creating the need for a "rescue mission"—an Organization of American States official who had left Grenada the day before the U.S. invaded reported more or less routine operations at the airport.[7] And even if the students had in fact been in jeopardy, some observers noted that if the United States made a regular practice of sending in the marines in the event of "violent changes of government in countries which contained American citizens," it would find itself "intervening and fighting continuously, all over the globe."[8]

In Panama too, the White House pointed to a threat to Americans as justification for military intervention. But if the United States needed to resort to military force to prevent violence against Americans in Panama, it had on the ground *before* the invasion "13,000 troops who were better armed, trained and coordinated" than their Panamanian counterparts.[9] Instead of protecting Americans, some believe the invasion of Panama "endangered U.S. civilians (not to mention U.S. soldiers) by leaving them vulnerable to hostage-taking."[10] Indeed, American civilians "remained unprotected throughout the action," and "nearly a dozen were taken prisoner and three were killed" *after* the U.S. invaded.[11] As for the death of an American soldier at a Panamanian military roadblock—an incident the White House stressed in its explanation of the invasion—the American seemed to bear some of the responsibility, as he had tried to evade the roadblock when ordered to stop.[12] Political scientist Abraham F. Lowenthal concluded, one day after the invasion:

> It is . . . spurious to argue that the threat to American lives in Panama . . . was great enough to warrant the use of 24,000 troops, the deaths and injuries of hundreds of people and the breakup of the structure of the local armed forces and police. At least until last weekend, American citizens lived and worked in Panama without intolerable risk. The isolated incidents that occurred then, and that are now being used to justify U.S. military action, were more a result than a cause of Washington's determination to oust Noriega from power. In any case, there were obviously many other ways, short of armed force, to reduce or remove the risks to those U.S. citizens.[13]

[7] Schoenhals and Melanson, *Revolution and Intervention,* p. 144.

[8] Illingworth, "Grenada in Retrospect," p. 132.

[9] John Weeks and Phil Gunson, *Panama: Made in the USA* (London: Latin America Bureau, 1991), p. 12.

[10] Ibid., p. 13.

[11] Kevin Buckley, *Panama: The Whole Story* (New York: Simon and Schuster, 1991), p. 241.

[12] Ibid., pp. 226–29.

[13] Abraham F. Lowenthal, "Are There Rules Just for Us?" *Los Angeles Times,* December 22, 1989, B7.

The threat to Americans in Panama, in this view, had not created a need for military intervention.

The second justification offered for the invasion of Grenada, the Cuban presence on the island, also sparked debate. The White House charged that a new airport under construction in Grenada with Cuban assistance had military purposes, but others observed that "British, European and American companies had been involved in the Grenadian airfield's construction, that Grenada had received direct financial backing from the EEC but *not* from the Soviet Union, and that a variety of Caribbean states had built similarly lengthy runways to support their tourist economies."[14] One study reports that "Non-Marxist Grenadians . . . stated that the new airport was vitally needed if the economy of Grenada was to show any growth."[15] A warehouse stacked full of weapons was discovered near the airport, but reporters found among its contents arms from the nineteenth century, suggesting that the military threat to the United States might not have been so grave.[16] As for the Cubans in Grenada, described in Washington as soldiers, in Havana as construction workers, reporters noted that "Many . . . appeared to be well beyond the age and below the physical condition usually associated with active military personnel."[17]

In the Panama case, there were questions in the United States about the extent of Noriega's participation in the drug trade, a major justification for U.S. intervention. The *New York Times* reported—three weeks after the invasion, when the Panama story had ceased to be the focus of public attention and had been relegated to the inside pages of the paper—that "far from [being] a drug kingpin," Noriega "appears to have alternated periods of involvement at the middle levels of the drug business with periods of genuine and zealous collaboration with U.S. drug enforcement."[18] In the assessment of one DEA official, "compared with other traffickers or even other corrupt officials in Mexico and Pakistan, Noriega was pretty ordinary—you're talking at most a couple tons of cocaine. Some guys move that every month."[19] Just as the description

[14] Robert J. Beck, *The Grenada Invasion: Politics, Law, and Foreign Policy Decisionmaking* (Boulder, Colo.: Westview Press, 1993), p. 30, emphasis in original.

[15] Illingworth, "Grenada in Retrospect," p. 134.

[16] Philip Taubman, "Senators Suggest Administration Exaggerated Its Cuba Assessment," *New York Times,* October 30, 1983, p. 22.

[17] Richard J. Meislin, "Cuba Assails U.S. on Casualty List," *New York Times,* November 3, 1983, A20.

[18] John Dinges, "Two Noriegas: Trafficker, Law Enforcer," *New York Times,* January 12, 1990, A35.

[19] James S. Henry, "Noriega Is Gone, but the Drug Traffic and Corruption Live On," *Washington Post,* July 28, 1991, C1.

of the airport, the arms warehouse, and the Cuban workers in Grenada as tools of Soviet imperialism had been open to question, the case against Noriega as a major drug trafficker appears to have been far from conclusive.

The legal critique of U.S. intervention in Grenada focused on the prohibition in the U.N. charter against the unilateral use of force except in self-defense. The Reagan administration argued that the Organization of East Caribbean States (OECS) treaty justified military action to counter a threat to OECS members, but one study reports that "When the OECS voted to take action on Friday, October 21, it lacked both Security Council endorsement and lawful invitation." This left "anticipatory self-defense" as a possible justification. "Yet such a claim lacked plausibility. What *immediate* threat to the OECS states could Grenada have posed,"[20] when no effective government existed on the island? Some found it even harder to see what threat Grenada could have posed to the United States.

The Panama invasion generated similar questions in the United States. Lowenthal asked: "Does any nation have the right to decide unilaterally—without invitation from a lawful and internationally recognized government and without approval in advance by any constituted international organization—to send in its forces to remove a foreign leader, however loathsome?" He could find "no provision in international law that allows one nation to dispatch troops to another with the mission of imposing democracy."[21] In response to the proposition that the United States could invade a country to arrest its head of state on drug charges, law professor Robert K. Goldman inquired (on the day of the invasion): "Can you imagine . . . how we would react if another nation asserted the right to have its military engage in . . . kidnappings of Americans in this country?"[22] Just as critics of the Grenada invasion compared the Reagan administration's citation of the OECS treaty in defense of U.S. intervention in the Caribbean to Soviet references to the Warsaw Pact as justification for intervention in Eastern Europe, critics of the Panama invasion argued that what the White House claimed to be a general principle of international conduct could not survive a turning of the tables with its legitimacy intact. U.S. intervention in Grenada and Panama, in sum, rested on similar justifications and was subject to similar critiques.

[20] Beck, *The Grenada Invasion,* p. 214, emphasis in original.
[21] Lowenthal, "Rules Just for Us?"
[22] David G. Savage, "Legality of U.S. Invasion Spurs Debate," *Los Angeles Times,* December 21, 1989, p. 10.

Debate in Washington

Despite these striking parallels, reaction in Washington to the two invasions differed. The invasion of Grenada received mixed reviews in Congress. Although *Congressional Quarterly* reported on October 29 that "most in Congress" had not criticized the invasion, Reagan's move divided the Democratic Party. Some "immediately charged it was 'gunboat diplomacy.' "[23] Senators Lloyd Bentson, Paul Simon, and Sam Nunn supported the invasion; Daniel Patrick Moynihan, Alan Cranston, and Claiborne Pell opposed it. A number of Democrats "had misgivings about its legality under international and U.S. law" and suggested that Reagan had used the medical students on the island "as a pretext to oust Grenada's pro-Cuban government."[24] Senator Christopher Dodd and House Foreign Affairs Committee chair Clement Zablocki offered equivocal support, arguing that the invasion could be justified *if* American lives had been in danger, but that more information would have to emerge before a judgment could be made. Walter Mondale, the front-runner in the race for the Democratic presidential nomination, argued that military action could be justified "if American citizens in Grenada were in serious danger, or if Grenada was on the verge of becoming a base for Soviet or Cuban subversion in this hemisphere," but expressed skepticism, observing that the invasion had made it harder for the United States to criticize Soviet actions in Afghanistan and Eastern Europe.[25]

On October 28, three days after the invasion, House Speaker Tip O'Neill positioned himself squarely in the critical camp, describing U.S. policy as "gunboat diplomacy."[26] This marked the high point of congressional opposition to the Grenada operation. Over the next few days, as it emerged that a nationally televised Reagan speech on October 27 and the grateful testimony of some of the evacuated medical students had boosted public approval of the invasion from 52 percent (on October 26) to 65 percent (on October 28),[27] Democrats toned down their criticism, their focus shifting to the need for more information on the events that had precipitated the invasion. To this end, a fact-finding delegation was dis-

---

[23] Richard Whittle, "Questions, Praise Follow Grenada Invasion," *Congressional Quarterly Weekly Report* 41, October 29, 1983, p. 2221.

[24] Ibid., p. 2223.

[25] "The 7 Democratic Candidates Weigh In," *Washington Post,* October 29, 1983, A12.

[26] Steven V. Roberts, "O'Neill Criticizes President; War Powers Act Is Invoked," *New York Times,* October 29, 1983, p. 1.

[27] Barry Sussman, "Reagan's Talk Gains Support for Policies," *Washington Post,* October 30, 1983, A1.

patched to the island. Upon its report that Americans might in fact have been in danger, O'Neill reversed his position, declaring on November 8 that "sending American forces into combat was justified under these particular circumstances."[28] On November 12, *Congressional Quarterly* reported "leading Democrats reluctantly joining the applause" for the invasion, although some continued to oppose it.[29] But the initial reaction of Democrats in Washington had been quite critical.

The reaction in Congress to the invasion of Panama is much easier to characterize. In the assessment of *Congressional Quarterly*, "President Bush received broad, bipartisan congressional backing" for the Panama invasion.[30] A few House Democrats criticized the move, but overwhelming majorities in the House and Senate expressed support. Although the Democratic response to the Grenada invasion was mixed, when it is seen next to the Democratic response to the Panama invasion the contrast is clear. Democrats in Washington offered a critical perspective on U.S. intervention in Grenada. No such perspective is found (except at the outer margins of the debate) in the Democratic reaction to the Panama invasion.

Research Design

For each of the eight interventions examined in chapters 3, 4, and 5, I conducted a simple content analysis of coverage in the *New York Times* and on ABC's *World News Tonight* and the *MacNeil/Lehrer Newshour*.[31] I examined the first two weeks of coverage of each intervention. The two-week period is designed to be long enough for critical angles that might not have been immediately apparent to emerge, but not to extend beyond the time that the intervention is a major news story and the focus of public attention.[32]

For the *New York Times* news section[33] and *World News Tonight*, the full coverage of each intervention was coded. The unit of analysis was

---

[28] John Felton, "After the Invasion: Support Widens on the Hill," *Congressional Quarterly Weekly Report* 41, November 12, 1983, p. 2360.

[29] Ibid.

[30] Pat Towell and John Felton, "Invasion, Noriega Ouster Win Support on Capitol Hill," *Congressional Quarterly Weekly Report* 47, December 23, 1989, p. 3532.

[31] On the technique of content analysis, see Ole R. Holsti, *Content Analysis for the Social Sciences and Humanities* (Reading, Mass: Addison-Wesley, 1969); and Robert Philip Weber, *Basic Content Analysis* (Beverly Hills, Calif.: Sage Publications, 1990).

[32] The Vanderbilt Television News Archive does not have ABC News for October 29, 1983, November 5, 1983, December 25, 1989, or January 1, 1990. Where possible, I made random substitutions: NBC for November 5, 1983, and CBS for January 1, 1990.

[33] By the "news section" I mean section A on weekdays, section 1 on weekends, and the Sunday "Week in Review" section, in each case with the exception of the editorial and op-ed pages. Other sections of the paper were not examined in the content analysis.

the paragraph of newspaper text or television news transcript. The major categories used in the coding were "critical" and "noncritical" of U.S. intervention. "Neutral" and "supportive" categories were not used, because this boundary was found to be extremely ambiguous. Coverage of military intervention is full of statements from administration officials describing the course of unfolding events and explaining American actions. Should such statements be coded as supportive of U.S. intervention, as they are presumably intended to be? Or should just those statements that explicitly endorse U.S. policy be coded as supportive? Using the first rule would produce a very high figure for supportive coverage, as government officials describing and explaining their policies are a ubiquitous presence in the news; using the second rule would result in a very low figure, as it is not so often that government officials *explicitly* endorse their own actions. As a naval officer quoted in the *New York Times* coverage of the bombing of Libya observes, explicit proclamations on the wisdom of U.S. actions are often unnecessary:

> An Air Force officer, asked how the Chief of Staff felt about the performance of the Air Force in the raid on Libya this week, stuck a forefinger into each corner of his mouth and pulled it into as wide a grin as he could.
> Naval officers expressed the same feelings about the navy's role, although they seemed a bit more subdued, as this was the second time in a month that navy aviators had struck Libya successfully. One quoted William James: "The best propaganda is the naked event."[34]

To avoid entering this forest of ambiguity, I have not tried to distinguish neutral from supportive coverage but instead have coded paragraphs as either critical or noncritical of U.S. intervention. While some ambiguities exist here too, they are far fewer in number and easier to resolve.

In addition to paragraphs that contain criticism of U.S. intervention, paragraphs that questioned one of the justifications offered for it were coded as critical.[35] In this sense the definition of *critical* used here is an expansive one, as a source who questioned one justification offered for U.S. intervention might have supported the policy on other grounds. The rule, in sum, is a simple one: paragraphs that express or indicate opposition

[34] Richard Halloran, "Hyperbole and Grins," *New York Times*, April 19, 1986, A16.

[35] Paragraphs just reporting that there are "questions" about U.S. intervention—as there always are—were not coded as critical, unless specific questions were reported that contradict official justifications or that otherwise suggest criticism of U.S. intervention. It should also be noted that paragraphs pointing out that the U.S. had turned its back on Noriega's drug trafficking in the past were not coded as critical of U.S. intervention, unless there is evidence that the source opposed the military action; most often the point being made was not an anti-intervention one, but instead: "We should have cracked down on Noriega earlier!"

to U.S. intervention, or question an official justification for it, were coded as critical.

Paragraphs reporting questions or concerns about U.S. intervention that were consistent with the position of the White House were not coded as critical. For example, some stories noted that the Panama invasion *could* turn into a quagmire if not successfully executed, an observation the Bush administration, presumably intending to execute the operation successfully, could hardly have disputed. Some stories suggested that the invasion *could* backfire if the U.S. failed to get a new Panamanian government up and running, also a position the White House would have endorsed (more on these stories below). This is the execution/outcome angle described in chapter 1; it does not question the wisdom and justification of the decision to use military force, but simply notes the possibility that the operation might not work as designed. Paragraphs *predicting* a quagmire, or *predicting* the failure of the operation, were coded as critical, as those who predict a quagmire are presumably opposed to the policy expected to produce it. Sources who declare only that a quagmire is *possible* are simply noting obstacles in the president's path, often in conjunction with advice on how to avoid them.

In sum, paragraphs questioning the *execution* of U.S. policy were not coded as critical if there were no questions about the decision to invade in the first place or the justifications offered for it. Nor was tactical or procedural criticism of U.S. policy coded as critical—this includes criticism of the president for failing to consult with Congress or for not explaining U.S. policy to the public in clear enough terms (ineffective public relations, that is)—in the absence of questions about the policy itself. It is paragraphs that question U.S. policy itself or the justifications offered in its defense that are the focus of the content analysis.

For the *New York Times* editorial and op-ed pages and the *MacNeil/ Lehrer Newshour*, the unit of analysis is the editorial, column, or guest. While stories in the news section and on the evening news tend to be constructed as a series of discrete, self-contained statements, opinion pieces and the comments of talk show guests are not so easy to break down into discrete units. Opinion pieces and guests that questioned one justification for U.S. intervention but endorsed the policy on other grounds were not coded as critical. To be coded as critical, an opinion piece or guest had to be judged *on balance* to be opposed to U.S. intervention. Although there were a few close calls, most of the coding decisions were easy ones.

I designed a simple content analysis in an effort to minimize as much as possible the element of subjectivity that is inevitable in this technique. To check the reliability of the coding rules, I had a research assistant (unaware of the hypothesis being tested) code 25 percent of the *New York Times*

TABLE 3.1

Perspectives in *New York Times* News Section Critical of
Invasions of Grenada and Panama

	Critical Paragraphs	Total Paragraphs	Percentage Critical
Grenada	291	3,524	8.3
Panama	36	2,185	1.6

news stories to check my own coding. The figures for intercoder reliability were 96 percent for Panama and 94 percent for Grenada. If the probability of agreement through random guessing is factored out, the figures are 89 percent for Panama and 87 percent for Grenada. I also had a second coder read a random sample of 42 *New York Times* editorials and op-ed columns from the Panama, Grenada, Gulf War (August), and Gulf War (November) cases. Intercoder reliability here was 95 percent, or 87 percent if the probability of chance agreement is factored out. The coding rules, in other words, appear to be quite reliable.

Critical Perspectives in the News

As Democrats in Washington were divided over the Grenada invasion but united in support of the Panama invasion, the indexing hypothesis predicts that critical perspectives should be easy to find in the news on Grenada, but relegated to the margins of the news on Panama. In the news section of the *New York Times*, 8.3 percent of the paragraphs on the Grenada invasion report critical perspectives not attributed to foreign sources,[36] against just 1.6 percent of the paragraphs on Panama, a disparity of about five to one (see table 3.1). About 1 paragraph in 12 on the Grenada invasion is critical of U.S. intervention, as opposed to 1 paragraph in 63 on Panama.

The tone and character of the coverage is best illuminated when stories containing 4 or more critical paragraphs—a threshold that excludes stories with just marginal critical content—are examined. As most stories in the *New York Times* contain 15 to 30 paragraphs, this is not a very demanding threshold. Turning first to Grenada, three such stories were published on October 26, the first edition to report the invasion. One focused on Democrats in Congress who opposed U.S. intervention. Representative Ron Dellums described the invasion as the product of a "cowboy mentality,"

[36] Chapter 1 explains why foreign criticism of U.S. intervention is not included in the main analysis. See below for a discussion of foreign criticism of the Panama invasion.

and Senator Daniel Patrick Moynihan questioned whether "you restore democracy at the point of a bayonet."[37] A second story reported the claim of the chancellor of the American medical school in Grenada that the invasion had been "very unnecessary" from the standpoint of student safety.[38] A third story on October 26 questioned one of the legal justifications the White House had offered for the invasion, the collective-security provision of the Organization of East Caribbean States (OECS) Treaty, signed in 1981 by seven Caribbean nations. As the United States was not a party to the OECS treaty, the *Times* observed, it was not clear how the treaty could have authorized American intervention. In addition, while the treaty provides for collective action in response to "external aggression," the White House had mentioned no external aggression. "Some experts," the *Times* reported, believed that "it might be difficult to justify the Grenada operation without setting a precedent that could be used to justify . . . the Soviet occupation of Afghanistan."[39]

The next day's *New York Times* included four stories with significant critical content. Two were brief and inconspicuous reports on antiwar demonstrations in the United States, but a third story made the front page. Although it focused on Reagan's explanation of the invasion, the story questioned a key element of the official justification, suggesting that military intervention might not have been necessary to protect the American medical students from harm.[40] A fourth story on October 27, the second in two days to question the legality of the invasion, reported that "some legal experts" found it hard "to distinguish the rationale given today from the so-called Brezhnev Doctrine." Even if a regional treaty could in principle override the prohibition in the U.N. charter against military intervention, the story observed, "It is difficult to believe" that Grenada, "when it signed the [OECS] treaty in 1981, intended to consent to being invaded under any circumstances."[41]

Critical coverage continued at this rate for about a week. One of two front-page stories on October 28 with 4 or more critical paragraphs reported that some of the medical students believed "Our safety was never in danger. . . . We were used as an excuse . . . to invade Grenada."[42] On

[37] Steven V. Roberts, "Capitol Hill Is Sharply Split over the Wisdom of Invading Grenada," *New York Times*, October 26, 1983, A22.

[38] John T. McQuiston, "School's Chancellor Says Invasion Was Not Necessary to Save Lives," *New York Times*, October 26, 1983, A20.

[39] Stuart Taylor Jr., "Legality of Grenada Attack Disputed," *New York Times*, October 26, 1983, A19.

[40] Hedrick Smith, "Reagan Aide Says U.S. Invasion Forestalled Cuban Arms Buildup," *New York Times*, October 27, 1983, A1.

[41] Stuart Taylor Jr., "Legal Basis for Invasion," *New York Times*, October 27, 1983, A22.

[42] McFadden, "From Rescued Students," A1.

October 29, a front-page story under the headline "O'Neill Criticizes President" focused on the Speaker's description of the invasion as a "frightening" act of "gunboat diplomacy,"[43] and a second story recounted the experience of an American who had flown off of the island the day before the invasion, when the airport, the administration claimed, had been closed.[44] On October 30, five stories with significant critical content appeared, one of which focused on the assessment of the Senate Select Committee on Intelligence that "evidence of Cuban activity in Grenada does not support claims that Cuba was on the verge of occupying the island or turning it into a base for the export of terrorism and revolution."[45] Two more stories containing 4 or more critical paragraphs could be found on November 1, seven days after the invasion.

In some of these stories, critical perspectives are overshadowed by the perspective of the Reagan administration. A story with 4 or 5 critical paragraphs, for example, might cite White House officials in 10 or 15, including the opening paragraphs that establish the frame of the story. It is clear from reading the Grenada coverage in the *New York Times* that the message of the Reagan administration was reported much more often than were the arguments of its critics. In foreign-policy news this is perhaps inevitable, as it is the executive branch that conducts foreign policy, and its words often constitute diplomatic *events* that demand coverage. When the administration speaks on international affairs, it is often not just explaining U.S. policy, but establishing it.

For this reason, my objective is not to measure the ratio of critical to supportive perspectives in the news and compare it to an ideal of balance, but to see if the media maintained *some degree of independence* from the administration's explanation of its actions. Over 80 percent of the stories on Grenada in the *New York Times* in the first seven days contained 3 or fewer critical paragraphs, and most contained zero. Yet three stories per day contained significant critical content, and about one such story per day was placed on the front page. Over the next seven days, the overall level of coverage fell, but seven more critical stories were published, including a detailed analysis and critique of the case for U.S. intervention containing more than 20 critical paragraphs. Although it is clear that the volume of critical coverage does not match the volume of coverage reporting the White House position, the evidence does indicate a substantial degree of media independence from the official explanation of U.S. policy.

[43] Roberts, "O'Neill Criticizes President," p. 1.

[44] Hedrick Smith, "Ex-U.S. Official Cites Ease in Leaving Grenada Day before Invasion," *New York Times*, October 29, 1983, p. 7.

[45] Taubman, "Senators Suggest," p. 22.

In view of the parallels between U.S. actions in Grenada and Panama, one might have expected the coverage of the two interventions to be similar. But in contrast to 32 articles on Grenada, just four articles on Panama contained 4 or more critical paragraphs. Of the four, two are brief stories just 4 and 5 paragraphs in length, buried inside the paper and appended to articles on other topics, that report criticism manifested as social deviance.[46] One begins with a description of opponents of the invasion in New York "Chanting angrily and waving placards" and mentions "heavy police protection."[47] The other notes three times that protesters in New York had "blocked rush-hour traffic" and conveys their message simply as "U.S. out of Panama!"[48]

Just two other stories in two weeks of *New York Times* coverage achieved the minimal threshold of 4 critical paragraphs. The first story, published on December 21, questioned the legitimacy of the new government in Panama, observing that while U.S.-installed president Guillermo Endara had won the election Noriega had nullified in May, "the moral claim of the Endara 'government' has weakened as the months passed" and could not have been greatly restored when he was sworn in "in secret, on an American base." The article also described White House officials as "obviously uncomfortable in trying to explain why the United States praised Moscow for its new policy of nonintervention and then intervened itself," and noted that Richard Nixon had expressed opposition to military intervention in Panama earlier in December.[49] The second story is an investigative report on the drug war in Latin America that begins with the observation that the Panama invasion might in fact hinder the U.S. effort to fight drugs in the region if it alienated U.S. allies such as Peru (the balance of the article is not about the Panama invasion). Too much should not be made of this article as evidence of independent reporting, however, as the critical perspective it contains is attributed to "Bush aides."[50] But these two stories and the two brief protest blurbs represent the extent of critical reporting on the wisdom and justification of the Panama invasion in the *New York Times*.

[46] On the media's use of a social-deviance frame in reporting mass demonstrations, see Gitlin, *Whole World Is Watching.*

[47] "250 in Times Square Protest Invasion of Panama by U.S.," *New York Times,* December 21, 1989, A23.

[48] "Protest of Panama Invasion Blocks Traffic in Manhattan," *New York Times,* December 23, 1989, p. 13.

[49] R. W. Apple Jr., "War: Bush's Presidential Rite of Passage," *New York Times,* December 21, 1989, A1.

[50] Joseph B. Treaster, "Battle against Cocaine Traffic Is Languishing in South America," *New York Times,* January 1, 1990, p. 1.

TABLE 3.2

Specific Questions about Invasions of Grenada and Panama

Question	Paragraphs Reporting Question	Total Paragraphs	Percentage Reporting Question
Required for Protecting American Lives?			
Grenada	78	3,524	2.2
Panama	2	2,185	0.1
Required for Stopping Communism or Drugs?			
Grenada	53	3,524	1.5
Panama	4	2,185	0.2
Violation of International Law?			
Grenada	36	3,524	1.0
Panama	5	2,185	0.2

If the two brief protest stories on Panama (and three brief protest stories on Grenada) are set aside, there are 29 stories (out of 228) with significant critical content in the Grenada case, against just two (out of 117) in the Panama case. This remarkable disparity is evidence of a powerful indexing effect, going far beyond what the reasonable efforts of journalists to report conflict in Washington as one aspect of the story might have been expected to produce.

Although the Panama invasion inspired questions similar to those posed in the Grenada case, the *New York Times* declined to cover this aspect of the story. Just 2 paragraphs in the news section of the *New York Times* questioned the premise that a grave threat to American civilians had existed in Panama, or that this threat (or the shooting of an American soldier who had run a Panamanian military roadblock) justified the invasion. In sharp contrast, 78 paragraphs in the Grenada case questioned the claim that the threat to American medical students on the island justified military intervention (see table 3.2).

Just 4 paragraphs in the Panama case questioned the wisdom or justification of invading a country to arrest its head of state on drug charges. In the Grenada case, the parallel justification—stopping the spread of Communism—was questioned in 53 paragraphs (see table 3.2). In the Panama case, 5 paragraphs suggested that the invasion violated international law. In the Grenada case, the figure is 36 paragraphs (see table 3.2). In sum, similar actions, open to similar questions, received dramatically different coverage.

TABLE 3.3

Perspectives on *World News Tonight* Critical of Invasions
of Grenada and Panama

	Critical Paragraphs	Total Paragraphs	Percentage Critical
Grenada	29	323	9.0
Panama	4	271	1.5

On *World News Tonight*, the indexing effect is no less impressive. In the Grenada case, 9.0 percent of ABC News paragraphs contained critical viewpoints not attributed to foreign sources. In the Panama case, the figure falls to just 1.5 percent (see table 3.3). Critical perspectives were broadcast six times more often in the Grenada coverage. Just 4 critical paragraphs are found in the Panama case: one in a story on the (otherwise supportive) reaction in Washington; one in a report on a press conference where Bush had been asked how he would explain U.S. intervention in Panama to Gorbachev (pointing to the contrast between U.S. policy in Panama and the Soviet policy of nonintervention in Eastern Europe in 1989); and two in a story on the impact of the Panama invasion on the effort to fight drugs in Latin America (where it is suggested that the removal of Noriega is not going to stop the flow of drugs to the United States).

The argument is not that ABC's coverage of the Grenada invasion was especially critical. Except for two critical stories the day of the invasion and two more the next day, ABC reported critical perspectives in isolation, inside otherwise noncritical stories. The objective here, however, is not to establish whether a standard of balance was achieved in the coverage, but to see if the media maintained *some degree of independence* from the official explanation of American policy. In the Grenada case, nearly 10 percent of the coverage was coded as critical of U.S. intervention. In the Panama case, critical analysis of U.S. policy was relegated to less than 2 percent of the coverage.

On the *New York Times* opinion pages, 12 of 27 editorials and op-eds were critical of the Grenada invasion, offering various formulations of the arguments outlined above. In the Panama case, just 2 of 15 editorials and op-eds opposed U.S. intervention (see table 3.4). Over 4 opinion pieces in 10 were critical in the Grenada case, against just 1 in 8 on Panama. Although not as great as in the news section, the indexing effect is powerful enough on the opinion pages to limit readers to one critical article per week on the Panama invasion, as opposed to about one per day on Grenada.

TABLE 3.4

Editorials and Columns in *New York Times* Critical
of Invasions of Grenada and Panama

	Critical Editorials/ Columns	Total Editorials/ Columns	Percentage Critical
Grenada	12	27	44
Panama	2	15	13

TABLE 3.5

Guests on *MacNeil/Lehrer Newshour* Critical of
Invasions of Grenada and Panama

	Critical Guests	Total Guests	Percentage Critical
Grenada	7	18	39
Panama	0	17	0

On the *MacNeil-Lehrer Newshour*, 7 of 18 American guests were critical
of the invasion of Grenada. Not one of 17 American guests was critical of
the invasion of Panama (see table 3.5).

Once more the indexing effect is dramatic: no opposition to one invasion, nearly 40 percent opposition to the other.

In sum, although it is no surprise to find that congressional criticism of
U.S. policy is reported, critical perspectives could increase from a reasonable baseline in the news when foreign policy emerges as the focus of political conflict in Washington. Or critical perspectives could simply be marginalized in the news if not first expressed in Democratic-Republican
debate. The evidence from Grenada and Panama offers strong support for
the marginalization version of the indexing hypothesis.

Foreign Criticism of the Panama Invasion

In chapter 1, I argued that criticism of U.S. foreign policy from non-
American sources does not have much influence in the United States. In
chapter 5, I offer evidence that the reaction of the NATO allies—perhaps
the one set of foreign sources that has real influence with elite commentators on U.S. foreign policy—falls outside of the spectrum of Washington
debate in just one case, the bombing of Libya. In the Grenada and Panama
cases, Western European reaction (as reported in the *New York Times*)

matched the reaction of Democrats in the United States. Three percent of the *New York Times* paragraphs on the Grenada invasion contained critical perspectives attributed to Western European sources; the figure for the Panama invasion is just 0.3 percent. Including criticism from the European allies in the analysis would simply increase the indexing effect.

If critical perspectives attributed to foreign sources outside of Western Europe were included in the analysis, however, the indexing effect would be diminished. Criticism attributed to Communist states appeared in 4.0 percent of the paragraphs on Grenada and 2.8 percent of the paragraphs on Panama. The figures for criticism attributed to (non-Communist) Latin American nations are 1.6 percent for Grenada and 3.4 percent for Panama. Overall, if critical perspectives attributed to foreign sources were included in the analysis, the indexing effect would be reduced below a factor of two: 18.8 percent of the paragraphs on Grenada and 11.0 percent of the paragraphs on Panama would be coded as critical.[51]

The reason for discounting the impact of criticism attributed to Communist nations (such as the Soviet Union, China, Cuba, and Nicaragua) is simple. Criticism attributed to official enemies is simply not credible in the United States, and in fact appears to *increase* support for American foreign policy (see chapter 1).[52] Latin America presents a somewhat more complex question, as the major Latin American nations are not official enemies of the United States. But in the one case (Panama) where there is substantial opposition to U.S. policy in Latin America but not in Washington, it is reported in the form of blunt declarations condemning the United States. Pitched to a Latin American audience, these statements are not phrased in terms that speak to U.S. interests and concerns.

Critics of the Panama invasion in the United States responded to the specific arguments the White House had made, claiming that U.S. interests said to be at stake could have been secured without the use of military force. Latin American opposition to the Panama invasion, as reported in the *New York Times*, does not address the issues and concerns on the agenda in the United States. A representative example is an article on the Panama invasion that includes the following assessments of U.S. policy:

Mexico and Argentina "condemned the use of force by the United States."

Argentina, Brazil, Mexico, Venezuela, and Peru "criticized the action as interference in the sovereign affairs of a fellow American nation."

Brazil "deplored the American action," called it "a step backward in international relations," and made "a vehement appeal that a pacific and an immediate solution be found for the crisis."

---

[51] Critical perspectives attributed to foreign sources other than those I have mentioned are found in 1.9 percent of the paragraphs on Grenada and 2.9 of the paragraphs on Panama.

[52] Brody, "Crisis, War," p. 219.

Mexico asserted that "the combat of international crimes cannot be a motive for intervening in a sovereign nation" and called for "immediate cessation of hostilities," stating, "The Panamanian crisis must be resolved only by the Panamanian people."

Chile "rejected" U.S. intervention.

Bolivia expressed "profound worry over the United States intervention in this brother country."

Costa Rica, Guatemala, and Nicaragua "condemned the use of force."

Argentina "deplored" the United States action.

Uruguay "rejected" the invasion.[53]

Reporting the reaction of foreign governments to U.S. intervention is an essential journalistic contribution. But stories on opposition to U.S. policy in Latin America frame the conflict as one between the United States and its neighbors to the south, instead of presenting the U.S. position as itself contested and open to debate. The tone of the Latin American declarations, moreover, is not one that could have been expected to change minds in the United States. Official declarations of foreign governments, presumably aimed at their own publics, are no substitute for coverage of policy debate inside the United States, if there is evidence that such a debate is being conducted.

The Invasion Might Not Work

If journalists index the spectrum of American foreign-policy debate in the news to the spectrum of debate inside the U.S. government, how do they maintain the impression that the First Amendment ideal of a press independent of government is being fulfilled? In the Grenada case the conflict between principle and practice is not so dramatic, as critical perspectives on U.S. policy—while indexed to debate in Washington—*are* reported in the news. It is the Panama coverage that demands an explanation.

The evidence presented up to this point indicates that critical American perspectives on the decision to invade Panama and its justification were marginalized in the news. But there is more to the story. One does find in the news critical analysis of the invasion *inside the terms of the original policy decision.* This critical angle does not question the wisdom or justification of the decision to invade Panama, but examines the possibility that existing policy, on its own terms, might not work.

The U.S. invasion immediately evicted Noriega's troops from Panama City, forced the general out of power and into hiding, and achieved other

[53] James Brooke, "U.S. Denounced by Nations Touchy about Intervention," *New York Times,* December 21, 1989, A24.

strategic objectives. For a few days, however, Noriega himself could not
be found, nor could order be restored in Panama City. One might have
expected journalists who "reinforce official power to manage public opinion,"[54] as Hallin puts it, and as the evidence to this point suggests, to have
presented the operation, despite these temporary obstacles, as the success
the Bush administration claimed.

On the decision to invade Panama, ABC reported just three critical
viewpoints in 14 days. Yet over the first 3 days of the operation, 8 of 22
stories on *World News Tonight* questioned the ability of the president to
achieve his own goals.[55] The day of the invasion, ABC focused on what
had *not* worked. "The key here," Peter Jennings declared at the top of the
broadcast, "is that Manuel Noriega . . . has not been captured." Following
a report that the Bush administration had offered a million-dollar reward
for information leading to Noriega's arrest, Jennings observed, "That's
an awful lot of money" and asked White House correspondent Brit Hume:
"Does that suggest frustration in the White House tonight?" Jennings
then wondered if "the operation, as well as the military says it's gone so
far, is a bit bogged down?"[56] While the decision to invade is beyond the
scope of critical analysis, ABC made a point of questioning the success of
the president in achieving the goals he had set.

The first edition of *World News Tonight* to report the Panama invasion
closed with analysis from Jennings, who observed that the "enormously
resourceful" Noriega had not been found, might once again have been
"underestimated" by American leaders, and could still be "dangerous."
In this context appeared this summation: "At the end of this first day of
operations, Americans are not quite sure what has been gained, or at what
cost."[57] If this statement had come at the end of a commentary on the
wisdom of the decision to invade Panama, it would have constituted criticism of U.S. policy. In the context of a commentary on the inability of
U.S. forces to find Noriega, it is critical analysis of the *execution* of American policy. "Americans are not quite sure what has been gained," not because the decision to invade is open to question and debate, but because
the invasion might not work.

The next day, Hume suggested to the president that Panama could turn
into a quagmire: "We really are in a kind of an open-ended military occu-

[54] Hallin, *America on Top,* p. 11.

[55] I counted the comments from the anchor that begin and end each broadcast as "stories." I examined a period of just three days because the critical angle under study in this
section is quite prevalent in the news; there is no need to examine the full two weeks of
coverage to get a clear sense of it.

[56] *World News Tonight,* December 20, 1989.

[57] Ibid.

pation now, aren't we, sir?" A second reporter observed that Bush had to be "frustrated" at the failure to arrest Noriega. ABC cited a poll showing 80 percent support for the invasion, but noted that "more than half [of those polled] . . . think the entire operation will be a failure if the U.S. does not capture Noriega."[58] Although American successes were reported, the pitfalls the operation had encountered were featured at the top of the news, presumably not what the White House would have wished.

This critical angle reached its apex the following day, when *World News Tonight* opened as follows:

> The summary of events in Panama today goes like this: Noriega still has not been captured; the fighting has not ended; the so-called dignity brigades, . . . who behave like goon squads, still roam Panama City. The Supreme Court was in flames, the Panama Canal Commission headquarters was a target, and so was the U.S. embassy.

"Yesterday, President Bush said the operation was pretty well wrapped up," the top story noted, but then countered that "he may have spoken too soon." Instead of an operation close to a successful conclusion, ABC described Panama as "a nation in chaos."[59]

The same pattern appears in the *New York Times*. Of the nine front-page and "news analysis" articles over the three days following the invasion of Panama, seven addressed the possibility that U.S. objectives might not be achieved. A front-page story on December 21 described Bush's decision as a "roll of the dice," warned that the operation "might end up looking more like Vietnam than like Grenada," noted "the possibility of a long and decidedly unheroic slog through the jungles and mountains of the isthmus in search of General Noriega," and suggested that the president "might be confronted, just before Christmas, with the awful spectacle of American soldiers in grim gray body bags being brought home for burial."[60] A front-page story the next day opened with "three major problems"—finding Noriega, getting the new government up and running, and freeing U.S. hostages—each of which could "diminish the success [of the operation], if not turn it into failure."[61] Other page-one stories cited "enormous problems" U.S. forces had encountered,[62] and described Panama City as "close to anarchy" and on the verge of "full-scale guerrilla

---

[58] *World News Tonight*, December 21, 1989.

[59] *World News Tonight*, December 22, 1989.

[60] Apple, "War."

[61] R. W. Apple Jr., "Noriega Must Be Captured, a New Leader Established in Power, and Hostages Freed," *New York Times*, December 22, 1989, A1.

[62] Andrew Rosenthal, "U.S. Troops Press Their Hunt for Noriega," *New York Times*, December 22, 1989, A1.

war."[63] A "news analysis" chronicled the efforts of the White House to "spin a war" away from Noriega's escape, and to "put the best face" on the Panama invasion.[64]

Despite the marginalization of critical perspectives on the decision to invade, ABC and the *New York Times* produced a substantial volume of coverage that matches a second definition of "critical." It is easy to see why journalists might be surprised to hear that there had not been critical coverage of the Panama invasion, as the news focused substantial attention on elements of the operation that seemed not to be working as designed. From the perspective of the Bush administration, it is easy to see why media speculation about White House "frustration" and the invasion getting "bogged down" just 24 hours after it started could be interpreted as having an effect other than "reinforc[ing] official power to manage public opinion."[65] To describe the coverage in these terms would be to overlook a major aspect of what journalists are engaged in.

But this critical angle is no substitute for the one that is *not* found in the Panama coverage. It positions the reader/viewer as a *spectator* to unfolding events, with the tools to predict how the operation might turn out, as opposed to a *citizen* with the tools to deliberate on the soundness of the policy decision that set those events in motion in the first place. It frames the *outcome* of a presidential roll of the dice as open to question, but does not present the *decision* to roll the dice as open to critical analysis and debate. What this critical angle encourages, in other words, is spectatorship, not deliberative citizenship. On balance, then, Hallin's claim that foreign-policy news has the effect of "reinforc[ing] official power to manage public opinion"[66] does ring true in the Panama case, despite the existence of substantial critical tension in the news.

Experts and Citizens on the Panama Invasion

To this point I have focused on the failure of the media to report critical perspectives on the wisdom and justification of the Panama invasion. But could such viewpoints have been found in the United States? If Americans outside of Washington joined the Democratic-Republican consensus in support of U.S. policy, it would be hard to criticize journalists for failing

[63] Lindsey Gruson, "Cities Are Looters' Jungles as Chaos Consumes Panama," *New York Times,* December 23, 1989, p. 1.

[64] Michael Oreskes, "Selling of a Military Strike: Coffins Arriving as Bush Speaks," *New York Times,* December 22, 1989, A18.

[65] Hallin, *America on Top,* p. 11.

[66] Ibid.

to report critical perspectives. There is evidence, however, that foreign-policy experts outside of Washington and interested, engaged citizens were in fact critical of the Panama invasion and spoke out against it.

As explained in chapter 2, journalists use three major sets of sources in their foreign-policy coverage: players (politicians and government officials), experts (former politicians and government officials, persons associated with Washington think tanks, and university academics), and citizens (the mass public, and citizens who show a real interest in foreign policy). Under the indexing rule, journalists consult players, Washington experts, and public-opinion polls. To increase their independence of government, journalists could also consult foreign-policy experts outside of Washington, and those citizens most interested and engaged in U.S. foreign policy.

In reporting military interventions, journalists much more often turn to Washington-based foreign-policy experts than to experts outside of Washington (see table 2.1). As I argued in chapter 2, foreign-policy experts operating in Washington (as a rule) offer analysis and commentary inside the terms and boundaries of Democratic-Republican debate. Experts outside of Washington, in contrast, are free to step outside the spectrum of official debate.

The major source of foreign-policy expertise outside of Washington is university academics. As there is no definitive record, one is forced to estimate the reaction at the time of university academics to the Panama invasion. To this end, I conducted a LEXIS/NEXIS search for newspaper and magazine articles and television and radio transcripts from December 20, 1989 through January 2, 1990 (the same dates used in the content analysis) containing the word *Panama* and also *professor, college,* or *university.* As it would be hard to cite a university academic without using one of these words, this search should have located most appearances by academics in the database. I coded each academic as either critical or not critical of the invasion under the rules of the content analysis. I excluded from the sample academics at universities *in Washington:* Georgetown, American, and George Washington Universities, and the Johns Hopkins School of Advanced International Studies. Out of 55 university academics found in this search, over one-third (20) were critical of U.S. policy. (The 55 academic sources,[67] it should be noted, are out of a universe of about 4,400 articles and transcripts that mention the Panama invasion in LEXIS/NEXIS, so this is not evidence that journalists often consult academics.)

Although there could be a bias toward critics of the invasion in the composition of the sample, in most cases it did not appear that sources had been consulted *because of* their critical views. A number of the stories

---

[67] The figure is 81 if sources who appeared in multiple articles are counted multiple times.

are wire service reports on reaction to the invasion in specific regions of the United States, where academics must simply have been the easiest foreign-policy experts to track down. On the other hand, there is a clear bias *against* coding academics *in the sample* as critical. Many of the sources addressed issues peripheral to the wisdom and justification of the invasion—for example, how to get Noriega out of the Vatican embassy—and offered no opinion either way on the soundness of U.S. policy. Although not consulted on the matter, some of these sources presumably were critical of U.S. intervention. The figure of 1 in 3, therefore, understates opposition to the invasion within the sample. As there is a possible bias in one direction, and a clear bias in the other, I believe the estimate of 1 in 3 is more likely to be low than high.

If something in the neighborhood of 1 academic foreign-policy expert in 3 had a critical view of the Panama invasion, it is hard to argue that critical perspectives were not out there for journalists to report. But what about the need for sound bites? Are academics incapable of framing their commentary in terms the media can use, offering instead abstract and obscure analyses? The evidence does not bear out this concern. Although some academics might have a hard time crafting sound bites, those commenting on the Panama invasion were often quite good at it:

"It's like the National Football League playing a primary school." (Morris Blachman, University of South Carolina).[68]
"The best you could say was that this is a controlled disaster." (Richard Millett, Southern Illinois University).[69]

Just as reporters prefer to interview those in Washington who deliver the most compact and punchy comments, outside-Washington experts who do this could also be favored as sources.

The idea, I should stress, is not that the press should grant special attention to critics of U.S. foreign policy, but simply that it should consult foreign-policy experts outside of Washington. These experts could be selected based on reputation in their field (see chapter 7), or in a more haphazard fashion, as is often the case in journalism. The one essential condition is that *reputation in Washington* not be the basis of selection.

A second source of foreign-policy opinion outside of Washington, of course, is the public. Although "poll results and public opinion are terms that are used almost synonymously,"[70] mass opinion polls are just one way to consult the public, one in which the opinions of the relatively unin-

[68] Joanne Kenen, "Experts Split on Whether Panama a Military Success," Reuters, December 21, 1989.
[69] Ibid.
[70] Ginsberg, "Polling Transforms Public Opinion," p. 273.

formed and inert masses can obscure the views of citizens who take a genuine interest in foreign policy (see chapter 2). A second measure of public opinion is the reaction of public-interest organizations that deal with foreign policy. Major national organizations such as the American Friends Service Committee, SANE/Freeze, and the Committee in Solidarity with the People of El Salvador (CISPES) spoke out against the invasion of Panama.[71] Smaller local organizations around the nation also opposed U.S. intervention. It is true that these organizations claim as members a small fraction of the American public. But in view of the extraordinary collective-action problem that citizens who organize to obtain a public good such as a noninterventionist foreign policy must overcome, the degree of organized opposition to the Panama invasion should not be regarded as insubstantial.[72]

If Washington debate is a powerful influence on responses to mass opinion polls (as Zaller and others have argued),[73] then some other method of consulting the public is needed if the "public opinion" reported in the news is to be independent of the government. Public-interest organizations are not representative of the general public, but this is precisely the point. The case for reporting their reaction to U.S. intervention does not rest on their size or representativeness, but on their independence of the agenda of issues and alternatives set in Washington. If a substantial segment of the foreign-policy expert community *and* major public-interest organizations are critical of U.S. foreign policy, despite a Washington consensus, journalists have evidence that issues and alternatives that deserve public discussion have simply been "organized out" of Washington debate in the strategic calculations of politicians (see the next section).

If the organizations opposed to the Panama invasion strike the reader as marginal or extreme, it should be noted that at the time of the Grenada invasion some of these very organizations were on the same side as the Democratic Speaker of the House and other influential figures in Congress. Although the Democratic Party made a political decision to end this alliance in the mid-1980s, SANE/Freeze, for example, not interested in building a political coalition to win elections as an end in itself, but in defending specific policy positions, reacted to the Panama invasion in 1989 the same way it and the Democrats had reacted to the Grenada invasion in 1983.

Further evidence of critical perspectives on the Panama invasion is found in letters to the editor published in American newspapers. A logical

---

[71] "Rainbow Coalition Press Conference on Panama," *Federal News Service*, January 4, 1990.

[72] Olson, *Logic of Collective Action*.

[73] Zaller, *Nature and Origins*.

place to look for letters critical of a military intervention under a Republican president is newspapers in relatively liberal cities. The *Boston Globe* and the *San Francisco Chronicle* were selected for this purpose. The idea was not to collect a representative sample of letters to American newspapers, but to see if critical public opinion existed in the United States where one might have expected to find it. Democrats in Washington declined to speak out against the Panama invasion, and a reading of the coverage in the news sections of the *Boston Globe* and *San Francisco Chronicle* suggests the same pattern of reporting as has been described in the *New York Times.*[74] But in the letters published in the *Globe* and the *Chronicle* there is clear evidence of a liberal critique.

In the *Boston Globe*, only 9 letters on the Panama invasion appeared in the December 20–January 2 period, but 7 were critical of U.S. intervention. To expand the size of the sample, I extended the period three days to January 5, on the assumption that the letters published on those days were probably written on or before January 2. From December 21 to January 5, the totals are 4 noncritical letters, and 12 critical. In the *San Francisco Chronicle*, in the December 21 to January 5 period there were 15 noncritical letters and 30 that were critical. The argument is not that the letters are representative of public reaction in general, but simply that critical reaction to the Panama invasion could have been reported if those citizens with the greatest interest in foreign policy had been consulted.

Each of the arguments against U.S. policy outlined earlier in this chapter is made in these letters. One letter asks: "How can protecting American life be a justification for the invasion when more than 20 men have died in combat?"[75] A second letter grants that "We have the right to defend our forces who are there under the current treaty, but I don't think that this action qualifies as a defensive maneuver."[76] Contrary to the White House claim that Noriega had declared war on the United States, a third letter notes that Noriega's exact words—"a state of war exists between the U.S. and Panama"[77]—were ambiguous in their meaning. A number of letters question the claim that the purpose of the invasion had been to restore democracy to Panama, noting U.S. collaboration with an authori-

[74] The editorial page of the *San Francisco Chronicle* supported the invasion of Panama. The editors of the *Boston Globe* offered a more equivocal assessment, noting that some of the criticism expressed in Latin America rang true, but concluding that the invasion might nevertheless have been necessary.

[75] Ronald F. Goldman, "Trying to Solve Problems with Force," *Boston Globe,* December 28, 1989, p. 12.

[76] Nancy Cornelius, "It's Suppression, Not Democracy, in Action," *Boston Globe,* December 28, 1989, p. 12.

[77] William M. Powers, "Panama Invasion Damages the U.S. Image," *Boston Globe,* December 30, 1989, p. 18.

tarian regime in El Salvador and U.S. ties to China. Other letters note parallels between the U.S. invasion of Panama and the Soviet invasion of Afghanistan; observe that although the United States claimed that Noriega's drug trafficking had to be stopped, Washington had supported "the Afghan rebels, who make money selling tons of heroin";[78] and argue that Bush had ordered the invasion to bolster his own image.

One of the letters notes a surprising contrast in events unfolding at the end of the Cold War in the Soviet and American spheres of influence:

> Just when the tensions of the world were beginning to relax, when the walls were tumbling down, and the possibility existed of a peace dividend from the reduction of armed forces, our continent explodes with a vast military action in Panama, in support of political differences.[79]

The merits of these arguments, of course, are open to debate. What is clear is that critical perspectives on the Panama invasion were not hard to find in the United States in December 1989.

The Politics of Military Intervention

While opposition to the Panama invasion could be found in the commentary of experts and citizens in the United States, Panama failed to generate the political conflict in Washington that marked the Grenada case. Is the contrast in the Democratic response to U.S. intervention in Grenada and Panama a function of objective U.S. interests, in which case the bipartisan consensus in Washington in 1989 might be said to have justified the marginalization of critical perspectives in the news? Or does it reflect a change in the political strategy of the Democratic Party?

The invasion of Grenada fell just two days after the death of 242 Marines in Lebanon, at the height of the Reagan-era Cold War. Democrats believed the public could be convinced that Reagan was irresponsible in his conduct of American foreign policy, and that foreign policy could be a source of political advantage for the party. The *New York Times* observed in December 1983 that "Most of the [Democratic] Party's Presidential hopefuls are . . . banking that their critiques of President Reagan's foreign policy will be good politics," and concluded: "chances are that foreign policy will hurt Mr. Reagan in the [1984] elections."[80] Aides to presidential candidate

[78] David Fairley, "The Real Story," *San Francisco Chronicle,* December 26, 1989, A22.
[79] George F. Amadon, "Another Cold War Militarization Must Be Avoided," *Boston Globe,* December 30, 1989, p. 18.
[80] Leslie H. Gelb, "The Democrats and Foreign Policy," *New York Times,* December 18, 1983, sec. 6, p. 50.

Walter Mondale believed Reagan to be "most vulnerable on the 'war and peace' issue and on the tensions that appear to be building between the United States and the Soviet Union."[81]

In this political context, Democratic leaders, including Mondale and House Speaker Tip O'Neill, tried to use the Grenada invasion as evidence that Reagan could not be trusted to conduct U.S. foreign policy. Over time Democratic criticism subsided, as the operation proved to be a success and Reagan seemed to be winning the battle for public support (although Mondale and others continued to question the invasion). But the initial decision of leading Democrats, consistent with their reading of the politics of foreign policy at the time, had been to oppose U.S. intervention.

By 1989 the political dynamic had changed. Not only had Reagan avoided getting the United States into a major war, but international tensions had dramatically declined. Meanwhile, Mondale and Michael Dukakis, like Jimmy Carter, had been defeated in presidential elections amid charges of weakness on foreign policy. After Mondale went down to defeat in 1984, influential Democrats concluded that the political viability of the party required that it appear more enthusiastic about using military force. The argument is explained by an adviser to Tip O'Neill: "There is a widely held view that the Democrats can't win the presidency unless they win the South. There is a further assumption that to carry the South, they have to project a more muscular foreign policy."[82] The Democratic Leadership Council, an organization of moderates formed to win back the "Reagan Democrats," argued that "southern swing voters have substantial doubts about the Democrats on questions of national strength and national defense, which remain important obstacles for the Democrats within the swing electorate."[83] Notice that the argument is not that there is *strong or deep public support* for Reagan's foreign policies, but that *one segment of the electorate*—Southern swing voters—favored a hawkish posture. After 1984, moderate Democrats launched a concerted drive to win over this set of voters, calculating that liberals would continue to vote Democratic.[84] As Southern moderates held the swing votes, an issue on which they objected to past Democratic positions began to be "organized out" of American politics.

[81] Bernard Weinraub, "Risk of War Rises, Mondale Asserts," *New York Times,* January 4, 1984, A7.

[82] Christopher Madison, "Democratic Tough Talk," *National Journal,* October 31, 1987, p. 2731, quoting Kirk O'Donnell, Center for National Policy.

[83] Ibid.

[84] This is consistent with the logic of the two-party system outlined in Anthony Downs, *An Economic Theory of Democracy* (New York: Harper and Row, 1957).

In the assessment of Senator Gary Hart in 1986, Carter and Mondale were defeated "in part because they were seen as 'not strong on defense.' "[85] Senator Lloyd Bentson urged that the Democratic nominee in 1988 had "better be a moderate [on foreign policy]. He's not going to win unless he is." Representative Dante Fascell perceived "a determined effort to show that Democrats support a strong defense."[86] In 1984, Democrats had seen political opportunity in foreign policy. As of 1988 the party had changed its strategy. But despite the efforts of the Dukakis campaign to put the new strategy into practice, at the end of 1988 the *National Journal* observed: "Many players in both [Democratic and Republican] camps assert that public perceptions of the party's defense performance have again proven an Achilles' heel for the Democrats, a disability that the party must overcome before it can hope to regain the White House."[87] It is in this political context that Democrats weighed the invasion of Panama, a high-visibility, symbolic action with the potential to have a major impact on the image of the party on national defense.

I encountered no evidence that the views of Democrats on the merits of military intervention changed between 1983 and 1989. Nor is there evidence of a significant change in public opinion. What changed is the electoral strategy of the Democratic Party. In response to the defection of a segment of the Southern electorate, the Democrats decided to avoid conflict over foreign policy and to focus instead on domestic issues. In this context one might have expected the Democrats to support a Republican military action almost without regard for its substantive merits, for this is what the political strategy of the party prescribed.

On top of this long-term strategic evolution, it should be noted that a more immediate political context influenced the Democrats in December 1989. In October, congressional Democrats had attacked Bush from a hawkish direction for declining to support a Panamanian effort to overthrow Noriega. In the words of Senator David Boren (representative of the tone struck by other Democrats): "For the United States, with all of our strength and force . . . to stand by—two miles away as the crow flies— and do nothing, and allow these people to fail, personally I think is wrong."[88] This put Democrats in a position from which they could not easily criticize Bush when he decided to act against Noriega, a point not lost on Senate Republican leader Bob Dole, who predicted on the day of

[85] John Abell, "Hart Won't Knock Bush—Yet," Reuters, April 28, 1986.

[86] Christopher Madison, "Searching for Consensus," *National Journal,* May 3, 1986, p. 1043.

[87] David C. Morrison, "Dogged by Defense," *National Journal,* October 29, 1988, p. 2722.

[88] Stephen Kurkjian and John W. Mashek, "U.S. Says It Knew of Plot, Denies It Had Active Role," *Boston Globe,* October 4, 1989, p. 1.

the invasion: "Many of the Democrats who were so eager to jump on President Bush in October are [now] going to be slow to do that."[89] Dole's prediction proved to be accurate.

Could it be that a change in objective conditions between 1983 and 1989—the end of the Cold War and the reduced risk of conflict on the periphery sparking a major international crisis—is enough to explain the Democratic decision not to oppose the Panama invasion? Although the argument might at first seem plausible, the problem is that if the historical record showed that the Democrats had *supported* Reagan in 1983 and *opposed* Bush in 1989, this too could be explained as the logical result of the end of the Cold War.[90] In 1983, the argument would go, Soviet gains in the Caribbean simply could not be tolerated. U.S. inaction in Grenada could have had major ramifications in the struggle to maintain "credibility" in the Cold War. At a time of heightened U.S.-Soviet tensions, there was not much to lose in the area of superpower relations. And Democrats who criticized the invasion of Grenada invited charges that they were "soft on Communism," a political position history had shown to be a perilous one. If the record showed that Democrats had *supported* the invasion of Grenada, this too could be explained as the logical result of objective conditions.

In 1989, the Cold War no longer magnified the significance of events on the periphery, and Panama itself posed no real threat to the United States. As the Soviet Union dismantled an empire, it could have been argued that the United States should have been at pains not to appear to be consolidating one. And Democrats had been liberated from the need to demonstrate their anti-Communist credentials. Democratic *opposition* to the invasion of Panama, then, could also have been explained as a logical response to objective conditions.

To understand why Democrats criticized U.S. intervention in 1983 but supported it in 1989, it is essential to factor in the changing political logic the Democrats confronted. If the party had gone down a different path in the 1980s—deciding to consolidate and expand its liberal base, or dividing more sharply along liberal/conservative lines—it is easy to imagine liberal Democrats having opposed the Panama invasion. Instead, while conflict over Grenada had been organized into American politics, conflict over Panama, with the strategic decision of the Democratic Party, was organized out. In the political context of 1989, Democratic support for George Bush's invasion of Panama could have been predicted without regard for

[89] Michael K. Frisby, "Dissonant Voices Are Few as Congress Goes Along," *Boston Globe*, December 21, 1989, p. 21.

[90] On hypotheticals in social science, see James D. Fearon, "Counterfactuals and Hypothesis Testing in Political Science," *World Politics* 43 (January 1991): 169–95.

the specific facts of the case. It therefore constituted weak evidence, at best, of the wisdom and justification of U.S. policy and should not have resulted in the marginalization of critical perspectives in the news.

In sum, media coverage of U.S. intervention in Grenada and Panama matches the prediction of the indexing hypothesis. When Democrats in Washington spoke out against the Grenada invasion, critical perspectives on U.S. policy were easy to find in the news. The Panama invasion, however, won bipartisan support in Washington, and critical perspectives were relegated to the margins of the news. In the Panama case, journalists offered critical analysis of the efforts of the president to *execute* the invasion, but declined to question the wisdom and justification of U.S. policy itself.

Despite the consensus on U.S. policy in Washington, critical perspectives existed in the United States, outside of Washington, for journalists to report. Foreign-policy experts at universities offered critical reaction to the Panama invasion, as did interested, engaged citizens. To explain the consensus on U.S. intervention that emerged in Washington, despite critical reaction around the nation, one must understand the political context of the 1980s, in which Democrats calculated that to win back the White House their party had to overcome an image of weakness on foreign policy. Because the Democrats had clear strategic reasons for supporting a Republican military action, whatever their estimation of its merits, the consensus in Washington behind U.S. intervention in Panama should not have been understood as justification for the marginalization of critical perspectives in the news. But because of the indexing rule, journalists reinforced in the news the political calculations of the Democratic Party, expanding the spectrum of debate in the news in 1983, and contracting it in 1989, as the strategy of the Democratic Party changed.

Four

The Buildup to the Gulf War

THERE WERE two major milestones for the United States on the road to the Gulf War in the fall of 1990. The decision to send U.S. troops to Saudi Arabia in August won bipartisan support in Congress. The decision to double the size of the deployment in November generated opposition from leading Democrats. The juxtaposition of the two stages in the buildup to the Gulf War, like the Grenada/Panama comparison in chapter 3, offers much insight into the impact of the spectrum of opinion expressed in Washington on the spectrum of debate in the news.

In August, the *Washington Post* reported that "members of Congress . . . were unanimous in support of Bush's actions." In the assessment of House Speaker Tom Foley, "Democrats and Republicans, House and Senate . . . are very strongly of the opinion the president had to act."[1] United Press International reported that "Democrats and Republicans joined together to support dispatching troops," and quoted the declaration of Senate majority leader George Mitchell, "It is important for the nation to unite behind the president in this time of challenge to American interests."[2] *Congressional Quarterly* found that "Every member [of Congress] who issued a statement on the U.S. military buildup in the Persian Gulf has praised the President's actions."[3] Although some in Congress urged that other nations needed to contribute to the military operation[4] and expressed concern that public support might be hard to sustain if a war started,[5] there appears to have been no opposition in Washington to U.S. intervention at this stage.

In November, Democrats were divided on the wisdom of the president's policy. Although Les Aspin, chairman of the House Armed Services Committee, supported U.S. policy, House majority leader Richard Gephardt "reportedly urg[ed] Bush to give economic sanctions far more time . . .

---

[1] Dan Balz and Molly Moore, "Bush Asks Nation to Back 'Defensive' Mission as U.S. Forces Begin Arriving in Saudi Arabia," *Washington Post,* August 9, 1990, A1.

[2] Gary Silverman, "Congress Applauds Bush on Iraq, Faults Him on Oil," United Press International, August 9, 1990.

[3] Carroll J. Doherty, "Members Back Sending Troops to Gulf . . . but Worry about a Drawn-Out Crisis," *Congressional Quarterly Weekly Report* 48, August 11, 1990, p. 2598.

[4] Michael Kranish, "Congressional Leaders Back Sending of Troops to the Gulf," *Boston Globe,* August 9, 1990, p. 18.

[5] Doherty, "Members Back Sending Troops," p. 2598.

before resorting to military force."[6] Senators such as Sam Nunn and Daniel Patrick Moynihan criticized Bush for moving too fast toward war.[7] In the assessment of *Congressional Quarterly*, "serious fissures" had emerged in the Congress, and "Bush was caught in what one member of Congress called a 'mini-firestorm' of criticism."[8] Some Democrats continued to back the president, but others spoke out against his dramatic escalation of military pressure on Iraq. Although Democratic reaction was mixed in November, the contrast to the supportive response in August is clear.

Coded as critical in these two cases were paragraphs reporting opposition to the decision to send U.S. troops to Saudi Arabia in August or to double the size of the deployment in November; criticism of the president for moving too fast toward war; calls for a negotiated solution to the crisis; criticism of the Bush administration for demanding an unconditional Iraqi withdrawal and demonizing Saddam Hussein to the point that compromise appeared impossible; and other statements that express or indicate opposition to U.S. policy. Also coded as critical were paragraphs questioning one of the justifications the White House had offered for U.S. intervention: the need to defend Western oil supplies; the need to resist aggression or defend Saudi Arabia; and the need to prevent Iraq from building nuclear weapons.[9]

As in chapter 3, tactical or procedural criticism of the *execution* of U.S. policy was not coded as critical if it did not address the wisdom or justification of the policy itself (see below for examples of this critical angle). Paragraphs that criticized the public-relations efforts of the White House—declaring that Bush needed to better explain his policy to the public—or that urged the president to consult with Congress were not coded as critical if they did not question U.S. policy itself. Although the definition of *critical* used here is in this sense restrictive, it is expansive in counting calls for a diplomatic solution to the crisis and criticism of the president for demanding a total Iraqi capitulation, arguments against U.S. policy that some who supported the decision to send troops could have made.

I used a second coder to check the reliability of the coding of a random sample of 25 percent of the *New York Times* articles examined in this chapter. The figure for intercoder reliability is 95 percent. If the odds of

[6] Carroll J. Doherty, "Uncertain Congress Confronts President's Gulf Strategy," *Congressional Quarterly Weekly Report* 48, November 17, 1990, p. 3880.

[7] Jean Edward Smith, *George Bush's War* (New York: Henry Holt, 1992), pp. 204–6.

[8] Doherty, "Uncertain Congress," p. 3879.

[9] Paragraphs pointing out that the Reagan and Bush administrations had not objected to Saddam Hussein's brutal behavior in the 1980s were not coded as critical, unless there is an indication that the source is critical of U.S. intervention; most often the message of such paragraphs is "We should have cracked down on Saddam Hussein earlier!"

TABLE 4.1

Perspectives in *New York Times* News Section Critical of August
and November 1990 Troop Deployments in Persian Gulf

	Critical Paragraphs	Total Paragraphs	Percentage Critical
August	60	3,756	1.6
November	154	1,951	7.9

agreement through random guessing are factored out, the figure is still a
robust 84 percent (see chapter 3 for intercoder reliability figures for the
New York Times opinion pages).

The figures reported in this chapter represent critical viewpoints *not
attributed to foreign sources*. This is because, as explained in chapters 1 and
3, non-American critics of U.S. foreign policy do not have much credibility
in the United States. The one set of foreign sources that might be an
exception to this rule, the European allies (see chapter 5), constitute just
1 percent of the critical foreign sources in the Gulf War (August) case.
European criticism reinforces the indexing effect in this chapter, as it appears several times more often in November than it does in August.

The News in August

On August 1, 1990, Iraq invaded Kuwait. Six days later the White House
announced a major deployment of American ground troops to defend
Saudi Arabia. Table 4.1 shows the figures for critical coverage in the *New
York Times* news section in August, with the November figures included
as a benchmark for comparison.[10]

Critical viewpoints are found in the *New York Times* five times more
often in November than in August. Just 1 paragraph in 63 contained a
critical viewpoint in August, against 1 paragraph in 13 in November. This
is evidence of a powerful indexing effect.

A more precise picture of the marginalization of critical perspectives in
August is painted when the critical articles one does find in the news are
examined. In August, 1 article in 40 contained four or more critical
paragraphs—a threshold that filters out otherwise noncritical articles with
a few critical paragraphs—compared to 1 article in 8 in November (the
average *New York Times* article contains 15 to 30 paragraphs). Five out of
201 articles in the *New York Times* in August contain four or more para-

---

[10] The dates included are August 8 to 21 and November 8 to 21.

graphs critical of U.S. policy. Two of the 5 articles, however, present sources who seem to have a conflict of interest. One article interviews relatives of American hostages in Iraq, who argue that "we went in too fast" and describe U.S. policy as "reckless."[11] A second article reports the reaction of Arab-Americans, who declare that if the U.S. is opposed to Iraqi intervention in Kuwait it should also be opposed to Israeli intervention in Lebanon.[12] Two of the 5 articles containing more than marginal critical content, then, frame the critics as having a special interest at stake in the Gulf crisis, one that might not coincide with the national interest of the United States.

The other 3 articles do not report critical perspectives inside frames that cast the critics as having special interests at stake. The first article examines the reaction of ordinary Americans; of the 24 views reported, 8 are critical.[13] What is striking, however, is that the eight critics argue, explicitly or implicitly, that the U.S. should do *nothing* about the Iraqi invasion of Kuwait. Three offer variations on "I say it's an Arab problem. Let's leave it to the Arabs." Two more make similar points, adding simply, "We have enough oil in this country to last us a while," and "We could get oil from Mexico." Two others suggest that the Iraqi invasion might have been justified. The eighth critic in the article suggests that U.S. intervention could generate international support for Iraq.

As an examination of public reaction to U.S. intervention in the Persian Gulf, this is interesting material. Yet it illustrates a major limitation of the "person-on-the-street" as a source of critical analysis of U.S. foreign policy. The only *alternative* to military intervention suggested in this article is that the U.S. ignore the crisis and do nothing, an absurd proposition. Not one of the eight critics so much as hints at a response to the Iraqi invasion of Kuwait other than U.S. military intervention on the ground. The alternatives, in other words, are framed precisely as the White House had framed them: military intervention on the ground or a retreat to isolationism. Other possibilities—offering security guarantees to Saudi Arabia, deterring Iraq with air power but not ground forces, working to achieve a negotiated solution to the crisis—are not considered (more on these options below).

This should not be surprising. A haphazard sampling of the opinions of ordinary citizens cannot be expected to produce specific policy alternatives that have not first been discussed in the news. For this reason, the person-

---

[11] Lisa Belkin, "For Kin of Trapped Americans, the One Word They Dreaded," *New York Times,* August 21, 1990, A13.

[12] Felicity Barringer, "With Loyalty Split, Arab-Americans Fault Hussein, but Question U.S. Too," *New York Times,* August 16, 1990, A16.

[13] Robert Reinhold, "Around U.S., a Cautious Chorus of Support," *New York Times,* August 9, 1990, A1.

on-the-street is not of great value as a source of critical analysis of U.S. foreign policy.

The framing of the alternatives as military intervention or isolationism, however, is not unique to the person-on-the-street. The second critical article in August that does not frame opponents of U.S. policy as having a special interest in the crisis examines the justifications the White House had offered for its action and finds them to be questionable.[14] One justification was to defend the price of oil, but the article notes that the U.S. let Saudi Arabia increase oil prices in the 1970s and observes: "The Iraqis understand the world oil market as well as the Saudis. That means understanding that if prices are pushed too high too fast, the West will find alternative energy sources, which will sooner or later drive the price of oil way down."

A second justification was to maintain (indirect) control over the oil itself, through Saudi Arabia, "the OPEC country that is more likely to cater to Washington's interests." The article points out that during the Cold War, "the stake in whose allies controlled what oil reserves had a military and strategic dimension. But today, with the Soviet Union cooperating in this crisis, that argument has lost much of its urgency."

A third justification for U.S. intervention was principled opposition to military aggression. Against this argument, the article offers U.S. policy toward the Khmer Rouge in Cambodia, one based on the very "might makes right" principle said to be intolerable in Kuwait. The article concludes that this argument is simply a cover for U.S. economic interests in the Gulf.

As critical analysis of U.S. foreign policy, this is much more enlightening than the person-on-the-street commentary just described. But the framing of this analysis undermines the force of its critique. Just like the article on the reaction of ordinary Americans, this article frames the alternatives as intervention or isolationism. Following an opening paragraph that questions whether the defense of Saudi Arabia is a vital U.S. interest, the negative view is presented: "For many Americans, the [U.S. interest at stake] is not clear. . . . [M]any people seem to share the view of Katie Safier of Miami, who mused in an interview: 'Why should we be involved? We could get oil from Mexico.' " The rest of the article follows from this premise, exploring *whether* the United States should be an actor in the Gulf crisis. What is not considered is *how* the United States should act. The journalist appears to share Katie Safier's sense of the alternatives: send ground troops to Saudi Arabia, or let Iraq overrun the Gulf states. The possibility that vital U.S. interests are at stake, but that other policies

---

[14] Thomas L. Friedman, "U.S. Gulf Policy: Vague 'Vital Interest,' " *New York Times,* August 12, 1990, p. 1.

might better serve those interests, is not addressed. The idea of defending Saudi Arabia with air power is not mentioned, nor is the potential for a diplomatic solution to the crisis. Iraqi intentions vis-à-vis Saudi Arabia are not explored, despite the fact that the focus of the article is on Saudi Arabia, not Kuwait. This is critical analysis inside the terms the White House had set; at no point does the article question whether the definition of the alternatives in Washington—for Schattschneider, the ultimate source of political power—is sound. The alternatives are framed as existing policy or nothing, action or inaction. There is no discussion of *how* to act, if inaction is not a viable option.

Although it might at first sound utopian to imagine that journalists could have weighed U.S. policy against potential alternatives, in fact it is inevitable. Politicians often outline intolerable alternatives to justify their decisions; on August 8, for example, Bush described the alternative to his own policy as "appeasement."[15] If the media report this, the alternatives are framed as existing policy or appeasement. If no alternatives other than intervention and appeasement are reported, the president has defined the alternatives. The question, then, is not *whether* the media should report alternatives, but *what* alternatives should be reported: Just those expressed in official debate? Or alternatives with support outside the government also?

One article in August does examine other ways the U.S. might have responded to the crisis.[16] Patrick Buchanan argues, "By using the Hitler analogy, Bush is virtually ruling out any negotiated settlement." George McGovern offers support for U.S. intervention but like Buchanan urges the president to "keep the diplomatic option open," although what "the diplomatic option" might be is not addressed. But the existence of an alternative other than existing policy or nothing—a negotiated solution—*is* noted in this article, as are the critical viewpoints of former attorney general Ramsey Clark, the antinuclear organization SANE/Freeze, the Southern Christian Leadership Council, the editor of the journal *Reason*, Coretta Scott King, Jesse Jackson, and two ordinary Americans.

Other than this, critical perspectives not attributed to foreign sources were few and far between in August. An article on August 11 noted that Senator John McCain would have preferred the United States use air power to keep Iraq out of Saudi Arabia, instead of sending ground troops.[17] The August 12 edition noted that a candidate for Congress in

[15] Smith, *George Bush's War*, p. 99.
[16] Andrew H. Malcolm, "Few from Left or Right Protest Bush's Big Stick," *New York Times*, August 21, 1990, A16.
[17] Michael R. Gordon, "In Just 2 Days, a Doubling of U.S. Troop Estimates," *New York Times*, August 11, 1990, p. 8.

North Carolina had questioned U.S. policy,[18] and reported that a poll had found that "4 in 10 Americans said [President Bush] was too quick to send troops" (more on this below) and "4 in 10 again said that American intervention just helped to protect the profits of the big oil companies."[19] Also on August 12, Senator Paul Simon noted "a second wave of public opinion which says, 'Don't let American troops get involved there.' "[20] On August 13, a college student offered the view that "I don't think you should ever fight a war," a rock guitarist declared, "It's making me sick. . . . I'm a serious pacifist,"[21] academic Edward Said charged that the United States had a double standard in its policies toward Iraq and Israel, and Jesse Jackson urged a negotiated settlement.[22] Finally, on August 19, Senator McCain restated his preference for the use of air power.[23] These critical viewpoints, however, appear in one or two paragraphs deep inside otherwise noncritical articles.

In sum, only 5 out of 201 articles on the Gulf crisis in the August period devote more than passing notice to critical viewpoints on U.S. policy. Of the 5, 2 discredit the oppositional perspectives with frames that cast the critics as having a special interest at stake in the crisis, and 2 more frame the alternatives as existing policy or nothing, military intervention on the ground or a retreat to isolationism. Just one article in two hundred, then, discusses U.S. policy in the context of realistic alternatives.

On ABC's *World News Tonight*, critical perspectives on U.S. policy not attributed to foreign sources in the August period number exactly three.[24] Over 14 programs, with 856 paragraphs of text on the Gulf crisis, the following paragraphs are critical of U.S. intervention:

Woman: "I would oppose it. I think the Vietnam War was enough."[25]
Woman: "If we put the money that we're going to spend on this operation into developing alternative energy sources we would be out of the woods in 18 months."[26]

[18] Richard L. Berke, "Arab Crisis, as Seen from Carolina," *New York Times*, August 12, 1990, p. 18.

[19] Michael Oreskes, "Poll on Troop Move Shows Support (and Anxiety), *New York Times*, August 12, 1990, p. 13.

[20] Ibid.

[21] Jason DeParle, "Despair, Calm, and Disdain Greet Mobilization at Bragg," *New York Times*, August 13, 1990, A1.

[22] "Many Prominent Americans Support the President's Action in the Gulf," *New York Times*, August 13, 1990, A10.

[23] Michael Wines, "Largest Force since Vietnam Committed in 15-Day Flurry," *New York Times*, August 19, 1990, p. 1.

[24] For ABC News, the August period is August 7 to 20; the November period is November 7 to 20.

[25] *World News Tonight*, August 9, 1990.

[26] Ibid.

TABLE 4.2

Perspectives on *World News Tonight* Critical of August and November 1990 Troop Deployments in Persian Gulf

	Critical Paragraphs	Total Paragraphs	Percentage Critical
August	3	856	0.4
November	21	344	6.1

TABLE 4.3

Editorials and Columns in *New York Times* Critical of August and November 1990 Troop Deployments in Persian Gulf

	Critical Editorials/ Columns	Total Editorials/ Columns	Percentage Critical
August	1	38	3
November	10	29	34

Reporter: "There was worry, wondering if this could be Vietnam again. But almost no dissent, just this in Cleveland where a couple of people in Mao shirts tried to burn a flag and found fellow Americans upset about that, terribly upset."[27]

As table 4.2 shows, the contrast to the November period is dramatic. Critical perspectives were reported on *World News Tonight* over 10 times more often in November than in August, evidence of a powerful indexing effect in television news.

Critical viewpoints were no easier to find on the opinion pages of the *New York Times* and on the *MacNeil/Lehrer Newshour* in August. Out of 42 editorials and columns on the Gulf crisis in the *New York Times* in August, 3 are critical of U.S. policy. Of the editorials and columns written by Americans, just 1 out of 38 is critical, about 3 percent. In contrast, 34 percent of the editorials and columns in November were coded as critical. The findings are displayed in table 4.3.

The two critical columns in August that were not written by Americans deserve a brief mention here, as their arguments illustrate why foreign criticism is discounted in this study. The author of one critical column is a British academic who offers no analysis of U.S. policy, but simply suggests a peace plan that requires Iraq to get out of Kuwait in exchange for

[27] *World News Tonight*, August 12, 1990.

"binding arbitration" of its territorial and financial claims.[28] Although this article is coded as critical because the idea of a negotiated solution to the crisis is contrary to the U.S. demand for unconditional Iraqi capitulation, the author does not address this enormous obstacle to the implementation of his suggestion. Instead, the burden is put on Iraq; the argument, in effect, is that "President Hussein must act quickly" to secure a settlement *the United States opposes*. No reasons why the White House should support this proposal are offered.

The author of a second critical column is a former Jordanian government official, who reports that the United States is viewed with anger and suspicion in the Arab world for its support of Israel, its vilification of Arab leaders, and the perception that "the West does not want friends but tools" in the Middle East.[29] Yet beyond this general condemnation of decades of American policy, the article addresses the question of what the United States should do about the Iraqi invasion of Kuwait in just one sentence: "One solution the U.S. should seriously contemplate is initiating an Israeli withdrawal from the occupied territories in return for an Iraqi pullout from Kuwait." No argument is offered as to why the United States should consider this idea. And the proposition itself strikes a dissonant note to an American ear: Is it in Washington's power to "initiate an Israeli withdrawal from the occupied territories?" This is a good illustration of why foreign critics are ineffective at influencing public opinion in the United States, as the argument is not framed in terms that speak to Americans.

Just one critical column in the *New York Times* in the August period examined what had to be the key question for Americans: What U.S. interests were at stake in the Middle East, and how could those interests best be served? Ted Galen Carpenter of the Cato Institute argues, "No one in the Bush Administration even considered alternatives to our barging into the region." Carpenter questions the equation of "a small third world nation" with Hitler's Germany, asserts that "Iraq's neighbors were quite capable of limiting its expansionism," argues that Europe and Japan could have provided naval support to a regional anti-Iraq coalition, and disputes the premise that Iraq had intended to invade Saudi Arabia. Carpenter criticizes the Bush administration for not encouraging the Arab states to resolve the crisis on their own and goes on to argue that even if Iraq remained in Kuwait, its interest would be in selling oil at prices low enough to discourage conservation and alternative energy programs in the West. Finally, he notes that U.S. intervention in the Gulf "serve[s] the interests of the national security establishment, which desperately needs a justifica-

---

[28] Marc Weller, "A Peace Plan for the Gulf," *New York Times*, August 14, 1990, A21.
[29] Kamel S. Abu Jaber, "Once More, the U.S. Misreads the Arab World," *New York Times*, August 10, 1990, A25.

TABLE 4.4

Guests on *MacNeil/Lehrer Newshour* Critical of August
and November 1990 Troop Deployments in Persian Gulf

	Critical Guests	Total Guests	Percentage Critical
August	4	70	6
November	10	27	37

tion for $300 billion military budgets."[30] The point is not that Carpenter is necessarily correct in his analysis; it is that his critique of U.S. policy is the only one on the *New York Times* opinion pages that speaks to U.S. interests and concerns.

The findings for the *MacNeil/Lehrer Newshour* are similar. In the two weeks following the U.S. decision to send troops to Saudi Arabia, 70 American guests appeared on the *Newshour* to discuss the Gulf crisis. Just 4 of the 70 (6 percent) were critical of U.S. intervention.[31] In contrast, 37 percent of the guests in November offered critical views (see table 4.4).

Of the four critical American guests, three appeared in a segment on the opinions of Arab-Americans on the August 7 program, the first to report U.S. intervention. Radio broadcaster Casey Kasem criticized the United States for opposing Iraqi aggression but not Israel's occupation of Arab land, and declared: "I'd like to see the President of the United States pick up that red telephone and call [Saddam Hussein] and say, let's talk." An Arab-American journalist asserted that "the problem . . . could be solved with . . . peaceful negotiation, and with diplomacy," and an Arab-American businessman argued that Iraq had legitimate grievances against Kuwait.[32] Writing on television coverage of the buildup to the Gulf War, Timothy Cook argues that journalists "did not use sources that they knew beforehand to be oppositional unless they were covered in reports that were segregated from the official voices heard at the institutional news-beats."[33] A similar point can be made here: three of the four critical guests on *MacNeil/Lehrer* in this period are "segregated" into a story that frames opposition to American policy as a special concern of Arab-Americans, not the national interest of the United States.

There is an interesting aspect to the timing of this *MacNeil/Lehrer* segment: it appeared on August 7, the day journalists first reported the deci-

---

[30] Ted Galen Carpenter, "Bush Jumped the Gun in the Gulf," *New York Times,* August 18, 1990, p. 25.

[31] Three critical foreign guests also appeared.

[32] *MacNeil/Lehrer Newshour,* August 7, 1990.

[33] Timothy E. Cook, "Domesticating a Crisis: Washington Newsbeats and Network News after the Iraqi Invasion of Kuwait," in Bennett and Paletz, *Taken by Storm,* pp. 119–23.

sion to send U.S. troops to Saudi Arabia. One could speculate that if the producers of the *Newshour* had realized what the story that night would be, they would not have booked a panel of Arab-Americans—presumably invited to discuss reaction to the Iraqi invasion of Kuwait in the Arab-American community—but would have turned instead to the national-security experts who dominated the program once U.S. intervention was announced. The existence of even this one critical panel, in other words, appears to have been an accident of timing.

The Perilous Gamble

Although critical perspectives on the wisdom and justification of U.S. policy were marginalized in the news in August 1990, it would be inaccurate simply to describe the coverage as uncritical. Despite the consensus in Washington, journalists found a critical angle in the possibility that existing policy, on its own terms, might not work. The press focused its critical energies, in other words, on the conflict between the ambitious enterprise Bush had embarked upon and the possibility that it might crash to the ground.

In the *New York Times*, questions about the execution of U.S. policy abound. Over the first three editions to report U.S. intervention, just 1 out of 16 front-page or news analysis stories contained a critical perspective on U.S. policy not attributed to a foreign source.[34] Seven of the 16 articles, however, examine the possibility that Bush might fail to achieve his objectives. The lead story on August 8, the first edition to report U.S. intervention, observed that "In making the riskiest move of his Presidency by sending American soldiers to a region that has proven a quagmire for other Presidents, Mr. Bush was taking [a] perilous gamble."[35] A news analysis the same day noted that Bush had "tied the United States and his own fortunes to a potentially explosive crisis with no clear outcome in sight" and predicted that "Bush's political fate may be on the line."[36] A story on August 9 described the president as "betting heavily" on sanctions to force Iraq to withdraw from Kuwait and characterized this strategy as "full of

[34] As in chapter 3, I examine a period of just three days in this section because the execution/outcome critical angle is quite well represented in the coverage; three days is enough to get a handle on it.

[35] Andrew Rosenthal, "Bush Sends U.S. Force to Saudi Arabia as Kingdom Agrees to Confront Iraq," *New York Times*, August 8, 1990, A1.

[36] Thomas L. Friedman, "Bush's Gamble in Sending Troops: Stakes Are Certain, Outcome Murky," *New York Times*, August 8, 1990, A9.

risk."[37] A second story that day (on the front page) notes, "The Administration has played down the fear of a hostage crisis," but offers the Iran
hostage crisis of 1979–81 and the political damage done to President Carter as a possible historical parallel.[38] In the "Week in Review" section three
days later, the *Times* warned that "there will be losers in the Persian Gulf.
It is difficult to imagine a resolution in which both George Bush and
Saddam Hussein emerge unscathed. . . . [I]t is easier to write scripts with
no winners."[39] The president was in a "perilous position," the *Times* observed, and was "betting the ultimate stakes," putting the United States
"in a politically volatile situation from which it may not be able to extricate
itself easily."[40]

The conflict here is clear and dramatic. The president has made a "risky
move," a "perilous gamble" for "the ultimate stakes." The president's
"political fate may be on the line." "There will be losers"—perhaps Saddam Hussein *and* George Bush—and the danger of a "quagmire" is great.
There is a conflict here between the United States and Iraq, of course,
but there is also a conflict between Bush's dramatic action and the possibility of disaster for his presidency. The focus of concern is on the execution and outcome of U.S. policy, not the wisdom and justification of the
policy itself.

One article stepped to the brink of questioning the decision to send
U.S. troops to Saudi Arabia, but then faltered. It noted the magnitude of
the gamble Bush had made and the potential for a hostage crisis or "a war
of attrition that would engulf half the world's crude oil reserves." It then
set out to investigate the decision to run this set of risks, but made it only
as far as the White House: "Tough questions, Bush aides admit, but, they
add, what choice did they have?"[41] And there the investigation ends, the
story having examined the risks entailed in American policy, but offering
an opening to assess the decision to set that policy in the first place only
to White House officials. Critical reporting is confined to the execution
and outcome of a decision that is, in effect, stipulated at the outset.

On *World News Tonight,* even this critical angle is not easy to find. The
top story on August 8 noted "the risks the President faces" in sending
troops to the Gulf, reporting that "the fortunes of the Bush presidency"

[37] Andrew Rosenthal, "U.S. Bets Its Troops Will Deter Iraq While Sanctions Do the Real
Fighting," *New York Times,* August 9, 1990, A14.
[38] Clifford Krauss, "Iraq Confines 38 Americans, but Their Status Is Unclear," *New York
Times,* August 9, 1990, A1.
[39] Andrew Rosenthal, "America Could Face a Long and Costly Commitment in the Mideast," *New York Times,* August 12, 1990, sec. 4, p. 1.
[40] Ibid.
[41] Friedman, "Bush's Gamble."

could hang in the balance.[42] Following a report from the Pentagon, Peter Jennings introduced ABC's State Department correspondent, John McWethy, with the observation that there were "other scenarios" than the peaceful resolution Bush spoke of at this point, and that "the worst is very bad indeed." McWethy declared that contrary to what the administration hoped, "it is far more likely . . . that Saddam Hussein will not back down without a long struggle," one that could involve hostages, a major war, even chemical or nuclear weapons. The contrast with the official explanation of U.S. policy—a defensive mission in support of the embargo—is clear.

Yet this critical angle appeared in just 2 out of 31 ABC stories in the first three days.[43] Television news is so closely geared to reporting unfolding events that *tangible evidence* of U.S. policy failing—such as existed at first in the Panama case, until Noriega had been captured and order restored—might be needed for this angle to get more extensive coverage. In the Gulf War (August) case, only a hypothetical possibility of policy failure existed, which may explain why this angle does not receive more coverage on *World News Tonight*, a program dedicated to documenting unfolding events.

On *This Week with David Brinkley*, a more analytical program, journalists offered several reasons why American policy might not work.[44] On the first edition of *This Week* to discuss U.S. intervention in the Gulf, Cokie Roberts worried about "the staying power of the American people" if the crisis were not soon resolved, and wondered, "How bad a quagmire can this be?" Pierre Salinger anticipated "a building up of Arabic support . . . in favor of Iraq."[45] The next week, Sam Donaldson argued that "Iraq doesn't have to invade Saudi Arabia" to emerge victorious, but needed only to "hang onto Kuwait. We have said that that's not going to be allowed, but there is no clear plan on what to do about it except for the blockade." For Roberts, time posed "a terrible problem," for "if the Iraqis hold onto Kuwait . . . and we just sit there for a year, two years, with a couple of hundred thousand troops . . . isn't the prospect of disaster great?" Donaldson argued that "as this thing stretches out, there are going to be morale problems" among the troops. Salinger worried that European support for U.S. policy "may kind of be slipping away."[46] On *This Week*, in sum, critical viewpoints on the ability of the president to achieve his objectives are plentiful.

---

[42] *World News Tonight*, August 8, 1990.

[43] Anchor summations that begin and end the program were counted as stories.

[44] No criticism of the decision to send troops to Saudi Arabia was found on the episodes of *This Week* I examined.

[45] *This Week with David Brinkley*, August 12, 1990.

[46] *This Week with David Brinkley*, August 19, 1990.

On ABC and in the *New York Times*, journalists found what appeared to be a political error on the part of the president when pictures of Bush on vacation were broadcast on national television as the crisis in the Middle East escalated. *World News Tonight* seemed to question Bush's decision to go on vacation when it observed that the president had "defended his decision to go to Maine with Americans stranded in Iraq and Kuwait."[47] The *Times* raised the same question when it reported on the front page that certain White House aides "would prefer it if [Bush] stopped speaking to reporters about the chilling Persian Gulf crisis while sitting in his golf cart." The *Times* pointed out that while Saddam Hussein warned of the apocalypse, "President Bush was shown on television this morning, fishing and grinning in the rain."[48] Finding no official debate over U.S. policy, journalists tried to start one over a possible error in the politics of its execution.

The *New York Times* also charged that the president had failed to communicate the stakes in the Gulf to the public, criticizing in one article "the inarticulate way the President and his advisors try to explain foreign policy to the American people."[49] It is clear from the rest of the article, however, that the *journalist* understands what is at stake in the Gulf and why U.S. forces are there. The article, in other words, is critical of the president as politician, not as policymaker.

The coverage of U.S. intervention in August 1990 turns out to be rather similar to election coverage. In election coverage, "the main story line typically focuses on strategy and tactics," who is up and who is down.[50] The focus of the critical angle found in the Gulf coverage is on the prospect that Bush could win or lose his "perilous gamble." In other words, it is on the struggle between Bush and the shadow of calamities that had befallen past presidents in the use of military force, instead of the decision to enter into this struggle in the first place. Just as election coverage "focuses on the *effectiveness* of campaign techniques,"[51] as opposed to the soundness of policy positions, the coverage under study here focuses on the effectiveness of the president in achieving the goals he has set, as opposed to the soundness of the decision to establish those goals as U.S. policy. If it sounds utopian to imagine that the media might have questioned not just the ability of the president to execute his policy, but the

---

[47] *World News Tonight*, August 10, 1990.

[48] Maureen Dowd, "A Grim Bush Golfs and Boats as Aides Fret about Image," *New York Times*, August 20, 1990, A1.

[49] Friedman, "U.S. Gulf Policy," p. 1.

[50] Daniel C. Hallin, "Sound Bite News: Television Coverage of Elections, 1968–1988," *Journal of Communication* 42 (spring 1992): 20.

[51] Ibid., emphasis in original.

decision to set that policy in the first place, note that this critical angle *is* found in the news in November (more on this below).

In sum, the coverage of U.S. intervention in the Persian Gulf in August 1990 is critical in focusing on the dangers that lurked along the road the president had taken, and in rebuking the president for not explaining his policy and managing his image more effectively. But while this might have been somewhat disturbing to the White House, which presumably aimed to inspire full confidence in its actions, it creates a sense of inevitability about U.S. policy itself, an impression that there is no alternative to the course the president has set. It indicates that the president is in a perilous position, but offers no basis for evaluating the wisdom of the decision to get himself into such a position. The coverage positions the reader/viewer as a spectator to the struggle of the president to overcome the obstacles in his path, instead of a citizen in a position to evaluate the president's decision to enter into this struggle in the first place. For this critique of the press to have force, however, it is necessary to show that critical perspectives on the decision to send U.S. troops to Saudi Arabia in August 1990 existed in the United States, outside of Washington, for journalists to report.

Public Opinion and Expert Reaction in August

In the aggregate, Americans supported U.S. intervention in the Persian Gulf in August 1990. A poll published in the *New York Times* on August 12 found that 74 percent approved of the president's handling of the crisis.[52] In view of the consensus in Washington on U.S. policy and the media coverage I have described, it is not surprising that most of those polled also supported U.S. policy. But while the polls registered support for U.S. intervention when respondents were required simply to support or oppose what the president had done, the polls also produced an interesting contrary finding. In response to the question,

> In its dealings with the Middle East, do you think the Bush administration has tried hard enough to reach diplomatic solutions, or has it been too quick to get American military forces involved?

just 48 percent declared that the administration had worked hard enough at diplomacy; a full 40 percent responded that it had been too quick to send troops.[53] As the *New York Times*, *World News Tonight*, and the *Mac-*

---

[52] Oreskes, "Poll on Troop Move," p. 13.

[53] John Mueller, *Policy and Opinion in the Gulf War* (Chicago: University of Chicago Press, 1994), p. 237. The poll was conducted August 9–10. The figures were essentially

Neil/Lehrer Newshour had essentially ignored the possibility that the United States might have tried to achieve a diplomatic solution to the crisis instead of sending troops, it is striking that 4 out of 10 Americans believed this option had been a viable one.

Offered a choice between supporting or opposing U.S. policy—existing policy or nothing—most Americans indicated support. But it turns out that a third option, a diplomatic solution to the crisis, enjoyed the support of 40 percent of the public, despite not having been discussed in the media. What this indicates is that a mass audience existed that might well have been open to the arguments of those who questioned the need for U.S. military intervention. But despite evidence to this effect from their own favorite research tool, the public-opinion poll, journalists declined to investigate a policy option that had no backing inside the government.

I have argued that to maintain their independence of government, journalists need to gauge public opinion not just with mass opinion data, but also in interviews with those citizens who are most interested and engaged in foreign policy, who otherwise disappear in the disengaged and uninformed majority. Most Americans do not think about alternatives to U.S. foreign policy unless others have inspired such thinking: for example, pollsters bearing questions about diplomatic solutions, or journalists reporting opposition to U.S. policy in Washington.[54] Some citizens, however, do contemplate alternatives to U.S. foreign policy on their own initiative.

Letters to the editor offer one window on the reaction to U.S. intervention of interested, engaged citizens. It is true that not all citizens interested in foreign policy write letters to the editor, and that not all letters to the editor are published. But letters to the editor do offer some general insight into the views of the most interested and engaged Americans, those who *volunteer* their opinions on public issues and express them in their own terms, not the terms a journalist or pollster has constructed.

As explained in chapter 3, a logical place to look for critical letters on a Republican military action is newspapers in relatively liberal cities. Once again I examined the *Boston Globe* and the *San Francisco Chronicle*, to see if critical public reaction in fact could be found in these liberal (but still mainstream) venues. The editors of the *Boston Globe* and the *San Francisco Chronicle* supported U.S. intervention, and in the news section critical viewpoints were few and far between.[55] The letters, however, were quite critical.

---

unchanged when the question was repeated August 16–19. Mueller's book contains an exhaustive review of polling data on the Gulf War.

[54] This is Zaller's argument in *Nature and Origins,* chaps. 3, 4, and 5.

[55] This is my impression based on reading the coverage in the *Globe* and the *Chronicle.*

In the *Boston Globe* from August 8 to August 21, there were 19 letters on the Gulf crisis.[56] Under the coding rules used in the content analysis, 8 of the 19 letters were coded as critical of American policy. In the *San Francisco Chronicle*, 30 of the 65 letters on the Gulf crisis in the same period were coded as critical.

The published letters, of course, might not be representative of those that are written. As the *Boston Globe* and the *San Francisco Chronicle* supported U.S. policy in their editorials, the editors might have made an effort to grant critics a hearing in the letters section; or the editors might have disproportionately published letters that reinforced their own position. It could also be that critics of a policy that wins bipartisan support in Washington are more inclined to write letters than are defenders of the policy. Fortunately, however, precision is not required, as the object is simply to establish that critical public reaction to U.S. intervention existed for journalists to report.

There are three themes that are repeated often in the critical letters. One is that George Bush had pursued his own political interest—creating a foreign enemy to distract the public from domestic conditions—or the interest of the military-industrial complex, instead of the national interest. Although this might sound like a "conspiracy theory," in fact it dovetails nicely with Zaller's argument that "Bush's political vulnerabilities"—centering on the state of the economy in 1990—help to explain his actions. This is supported by other studies Zaller cites that explain U.S. intervention as a function of domestic economic conditions. Zaller concludes: "U.S. presidents from Truman to Reagan have, in fact, been more prone to use force at times when the country was in economic difficulty."[57] If this is a conspiracy theory, it is one that has social science behind it.

A second theme of the letters is that the White House had been hypocritical in professing moral outrage at the Iraqi invasion of Kuwait. Several letters noted America's own record of invading other countries and tolerating invasions conducted by its allies, and argued that Washington's outrage in this case rested on dubious moral ground. A third theme of the letters is that a new U.S. energy policy would be a more effective response to the crisis than military action. Some noted that higher oil prices might end up costing less than a war against Iraq; others observed that higher oil prices could have the positive effect of encouraging investment in new sources of energy. In sum, a range of arguments against U.S. policy are found in the letters to the *Boston Globe* and the *San Francisco*

[56] A few were written before August 8 but anticipate military intervention.

[57] John Zaller, "Strategic Politicians, Public Opinion, and the Gulf Crisis," in Bennett and Paletz, *Taken by Storm*, p. 255.

Chronicle, arguments that are ignored or marginalized in the coverage examined above.

Further evidence of this nature is found on the August 17 edition of the *MacNeil/Lehrer Newshour*. The *Newshour* asked its panel of newspaper editors—who supported U.S. policy themselves—about the reaction of their readers to U.S. intervention in the Persian Gulf. The editors reported general support for the president, but noted that other currents of opinion existed. James Goldsborough of the *San Jose Mercury News* told the *Newshour:* "we certainly supported the President's decision, particularly after the Saudis asked us to go in, but interestingly, I've looked to the letters to the editor that we've received over the last couple of days, and the opinion in those letters to the editor is about 20 to 15 against." While distancing himself from the opinions expressed in the letters, Goldsborough reported "three currents that were skeptical of our action." One current argued, "why save our oil supply when that's ruining the environment?" A second opposed the use of military force in general, and a third saw hypocrisy in the U.S. reaction to Iraq's invasion of Kuwait, when "we tolerate Israel's presence in Arab lands."[58]

Other editors on the panel reported opposition in their communities. Jane Marcham of the *Ithaca Journal* spoke of "a lot of skepticism, a lot of worry, a lot of feeling we shouldn't be there at all, or at least negotiations should be the route." Clarence Page of the *Chicago Tribune*, although he also reported much support for U.S. policy, noted that some readers were wondering, "why are we defending one kingdom in order to try to retrieve another kingdom for the Emir of Kuwait?" Gerald Warren of the *San Diego Union* reported that some readers were "questioning why we are going in there to defend a 15 cent oil price or to defend the monarchy in Saudi Arabia."[59]

The editors consulted on the *Newshour*, in sum, reported five arguments against U.S. policy their readers had made: Why risk war for oil that harms the environment? Why risk war over the price of oil? Why risk war to defend a monarchy? Why resist aggression in Kuwait if not elsewhere? Why not look for a diplomatic solution instead of sending troops? But despite this evidence of opposition to U.S. intervention around the country, the critics themselves were not interviewed on the *Newshour*. Instead, their views were filtered through newspaper editors who supported U.S. policy, who reported them not as serious arguments against U.S. intervention that needed to be engaged, but simply as evidence that some Americans had not yet joined the consensus.

[58] *MacNeil/Lehrer Newshour*, August 17, 1990.
[59] Ibid.

A second source of evidence that citizens interested in U.S. foreign policy questioned the wisdom of military intervention in the Persian Gulf is the reaction of public-interest organizations. The national antinuclear organization SANE/Freeze issued a statement on August 16 declaring: "A needless military confrontation is being provoked by an administration which has failed to exhaust the opportunities for negotiation." The statement went on to question "the conclusion that U.S. national security is at risk," and "the increasing appeals to the memory of the outbreak of World War II."[60] As of August 21, the American Friends Service Committee, a second national peace organization, had written to the administration "urging that diplomacy be employed to seek a resolution" of the crisis.[61] In California, the Los Angeles Coalition Against U.S. Intervention in the Middle East, composed of 35 peace organizations, had formed.[62] Also emerging in August were the Florida Coalition for Peace and Justice, composed of "65 peace groups and church committees in 40 cities,"[63] the Emergency Committee to Stop the U.S. War in the Middle East (in San Francisco),[64] the Long Island Alliance for Peaceful Alternatives (in New York),[65] and other local and regional organizations.

I argued in chapter 2 that because of the natural barriers citizens who endeavor to organize in pursuit of a public good of the nature of a noninterventionist foreign policy must overcome, the modest size of some of these organizations should not be ground for rejecting their claim to space in the public sphere.[66] If there were no other evidence of critical reaction to U.S. intervention, a case might be made for discounting the significance of public-interest organizations. It is the accumulation of evidence—the letters to the editor, the surprising piece of polling data, the reaction of foreign-policy experts (see below), *and* the reaction of public-interest organizations—that supports the conclusion that a substantial volume of critical reaction existed in the United States for journalists to report.

Critical perspectives on U.S. intervention were also found in the reaction of foreign-policy experts in August 1990. While the Washington foreign-policy establishment offered the White House near-unanimous

[60] "SANE/Freeze Statement on Iraq Invasion and U.S. Response," *U.S. Newswire,* August 16, 1990.

[61] Garry Abrams, "Activists Find Peace a Hard Sell," *Los Angeles Times,* August 22, 1990, E1.

[62] Ibid.

[63] Karen Samsock, "Peace Activists Beginning to Stir," *Orlando Sentinel Tribune,* August 25, 1990, A9.

[64] Nanette Asimov, "Anti-War Forces Rally in Gulf Crisis," *San Francisco Chronicle,* August 28, 1990, A13.

[65] Irving Long, "Pursuing Peace," *Newsday,* August 29, 1990, p. 30.

[66] Olson, *Logic of Collective Action.*

support, experts outside of Washington engaged in a much more diverse debate. As evidence of this, I conducted a search for academic experts mentioned in the LEXIS/NEXIS database (see chapter 3 for details on the method) in the 14-day period under study and coded them as either critical of U.S. policy or noncritical under the rules of the content analysis. As in chapter 3, I excluded from the sample academics working at universities *in Washington:* Georgetown, George Washington, and American Universities, and the Johns Hopkins School of Advanced International Studies. Of the 127 outside-Washington academic experts located in this search, 22 percent (28) were coded as critical. (As in the Panama case, this is *not* evidence of significant journalistic use of academic sources, as the 127[67] sources are from a universe of over 15,000 articles on the Gulf crisis.)

The figure of 22 percent is smaller than the 36 percent figure in the Panama case. But even in August 1990, almost one academic in four in the LEXIS/NEXIS database was critical of U.S. policy. As in the Panama case, there is a possible bias in this figure in one direction, and a definite bias in the other. If journalists consulted certain academics *because of* their critical views on American policy (there is no evidence of this, but it might be the case), the sample would overrepresent critics. There is, however, a definite bias in the opposite direction: well over half of the sources in the sample offered no opinion either way on U.S. policy, commenting instead on the mechanics of the sanctions, the nature of the Iraqi economy, the orientation of Iran, or some other topic that did not entail expressing a position on the wisdom and justification of U.S. policy. This introduces a clear bias against coding sources *in the sample* as critical.

As sources who questioned the wisdom of the president's demand for an unconditional Iraqi capitulation are counted as critical of U.S. policy in this study, the figure of 22 percent is almost certain to be low. American journalists marginalized this aspect of the story, framing the alternatives as intervention on the ground or isolationism, instead of examining the specific policy U.S. troops supported (Iraq must capitulate without conditions). Most of the academic experts found in the LEXIS/NEXIS database had no chance to weigh in on the idea of a diplomatic resolution of the crisis, as this is not what journalists were investigating. Fortunately, the objective here is not to offer a precise measure of expert reaction to U.S. policy in August 1990, but simply to establish that critical viewpoints could have been found if journalists had interviewed foreign-policy experts inside *and outside* of Washington.

In sum, the assessment of the *Washington Post* that U.S. intervention had the support of "a political consensus on foreign policy not seen since

---

[67] The figure is 246 if sources appearing in multiple articles are counted multiple times.

Pearl Harbor"[68] might well have described the public reaction of official Washington, but it does not describe the reaction of foreign-policy experts and interested, engaged citizens outside of Washington, despite extraordinarily uncritical media coverage. Even in Washington, there is more to the story than has been indicated to this point. Until the White House decided on a military response, leading Democrats in the House and Senate *opposed* the idea of sending U.S. troops to the Middle East in response to the Iraqi invasion of Kuwait.

The Politics of August

Does the consensus in Washington on U.S. intervention in the Persian Gulf in August 1990 constitute justification for the decision of the media to marginalize critical perspectives outside of Washington? If Democrats had concerns about U.S. policy in August, they also had clear incentives not to express their concerns in public. In response to the defeat of Democratic candidates seen as weak on military and defense issues in the presidential elections of 1980, 1984, and 1988, the Democratic Party had made a great effort to appear more hawkish (see chapter 3). This must have discouraged Democrats in August 1990 from questioning a Republican decision to use military force. Zaller reports that "Democratic aides conceded that their party's reputation for weakness was a constraining factor in the calculations of the House leadership" in the period before the Gulf War.[69] Seeing their greatest strength in domestic policy, Democrats could use the Gulf crisis to help neutralize the negative image of their party on defense issues by supporting a Republican intervention.

Questioning the decision to send American troops to Saudi Arabia would have entailed major political risks. Democratic opposition to U.S. intervention would have reignited charges that the party lacked the fortitude to use the military to defend American interests. In November, as I explain below, Democrats confronted a less restrictive political situation. In August, however, Democratic opposition to U.S. intervention would have made no political sense.

[68] E. J. Dionne Jr., "Post–Cold War Consensus Backs U.S. Intervention," *Washington Post,* August 8, 1990, A12.

[69] Zaller, "Strategic Politicians," p. 271. Zaller does not see politics as a major influence on the reaction of the Democrats to U.S. intervention in August. Although he offers a nuanced argument for the influence of political calculations on President Bush's decision to send troops to the Persian Gulf, Zaller concludes that Democrats rallied behind the president "on the basis of their own convictions" (p. 257). But the political context in August should have had as much influence on Democrats as (in Zaller's view) it had on the president.

The immediate political context of August 1990 offered further reason for Democrats who might have questioned the wisdom of U.S. policy in the Persian Gulf not to speak out. The Democratic Congress and the Bush administration were in the midst of the political battle that produced the 1990 budget deal in which the president went back on his famous "no new taxes" pledge, a decision that would come back to haunt him in 1992. In August 1990, the Democrats could sense the strength of their political position on this cluster of domestic issues; *Time* magazine described Democrats as "gloating" over their political maneuvering in the budget talks. As House Ways and Means Committee chairman Dan Rostenkowski explained the politics of the situation: "The Republicans have just shot themselves in the foot, in the neck, in the ear. They're masochists."[70] Expecting to score major political points in the budget talks, the last thing Democrats wanted was for the focus of political conflict to shift into the foreign-policy arena. It is in this context that the reaction of Democrats to U.S. intervention must be understood.

While the charge that elected officials act on the basis of strategic calculations can conjure up images of unscrupulous politicians supporting dubious policies just to win votes, politicians need not go against their convictions to be acting on political motives. They need only resolve uncertainty in a direction consistent with the political logic they confront. As Zaller observes, "decision-makers need not be aware of their real motives . . . in order to have been influenced by politics. They can simply allow themselves, possibly unconsciously, to be persuaded by reasons that someone else, in different political circumstances, would not find persuasive."[71] For a Democratic Party interested in appearing resolute on foreign and defense policy and keeping the focus of political conflict in Washington on domestic issues, the political path of least resistance was to support the president in the use of force, whatever their view of the merits of his policy.

Expectations about the future course of events must also have encouraged Democrats to support the president in August. A dilemma loomed for the president: if Iraq refused to back down, Bush could be expected to confront on one horn a public demanding a resolution to the crisis, and on the other a war that few expected to be as easy or as popular as it turned out to be. Either way, Democrats could anticipate trouble for the president down the road without having to contribute to its creation.

If President Bush or the Republican Party had had an image of excessive hawkishness—as President Reagan had in 1983—and if the Democrats had not been engaged in an ongoing effort to strike a hawkish pose, the

---

[70] Michael Duffy, "A Deficit of Guts," *Time,* August 13, 1990, p. 32.
[71] Zaller, "Strategic Politicians," pp. 254–55.

Democratic response might well have been more critical. In 1983, Democrats opposed the invasion of Grenada. In 1993 and 1994, with Clinton seen in some circles as unfit to be commander in chief, and the Republicans established as the party of Grenada, Panama, and the Gulf War, Republicans opposed U.S. actions in Somalia and Haiti (see chapter 5). The argument is not that the opposition party invariably supports the use of military force, but that Democrats in 1990 had *specific reasons to resolve uncertainty in this direction.*

The most striking evidence that political calculations influenced the Democratic response to U.S. intervention is found in the statements of congressional Democrats after Iraq invaded Kuwait on August 1, but before the White House decided to send troops to Saudi Arabia on August 7. Between August 1 and August 7, top Democrats spoke out against a military response, a position that disappeared quite suddenly once the White House announced its policy. Although the *Boston Globe* reported on August 3 that "Many members of Congress, from the most liberal to most conservative, suggested that military force might have to be used,"[72] an impressive list of Democratic foreign-policy experts argued otherwise.

On August 3, Lee Hamilton, whom the *New York Times* in 1990 described as "his party's point man on foreign affairs in the House,"[73] stated this position in no uncertain terms: "Until he [Saddam Hussein] does that [invades Saudi Arabia], I think it would be a mistake to commit . . . military power, and I think that the United States should pursue and is pursuing a course of political and diplomatic and economic isolation of Iraq. That's the course I think we're on, and I think that's the correct course."[74] Echoing Hamilton, Sam Nunn, chairman of the Senate Armed Services Committee, asserted: "I don't think we have a military option at the moment, nor do we have a treaty obligation. . . . I believe that our primary recourse should be to very intensive diplomatic activity."[75] David Boren, chairman of the Senate Intelligence Committee, argued that "it would be imprudent of the President to immediately commit American forces."[76] Senator Alan Cranston declared that even if Iraq invaded Saudi Arabia, "I see little possibility of American troops being sent (to fight) on Saudi soil, but there are other military options . . . naval or

[72] Michael Kranish, "Congress Backs Sanctions against Iraq," *Boston Globe,* August 3, 1990, p. 3.

[73] R. W. Apple Jr., "Hostage Decision and U.S. Doubts May Give Iraq a New Edge," *New York Times,* December 9, 1990, sec. 4, p. 1.

[74] *Nightline,* August 3, 1990.

[75] Michael R. Gordon, "Iraq's Advantage Limits U.S. Options," *New York Times,* August 3, 1990, A1.

[76] *MacNeil/Lehrer Newshour,* August 2, 1990.

air . . . that we could undertake."[77] In sum, before Bush had sent troops to Saudi Arabia, Democrats in Congress argued against a military response. Once Bush made his decision, however, this position vanished from Washington debate.

Could information that emerged between August 1 and August 7 have caused Hamilton, Nunn, Boren, and Cranston to change their minds? The argument the White House used on August 8 to explain its decision was that Iraqi forces had massed on the Saudi border in a "menacing posture."[78] Yet the administration's own reports were equivocal; far from revealing preparations for an Iraqi invasion of Saudi Arabia, they simply indicated that this was *possible*, as it had been on August 1. The reports, moreover, pointed to the conclusion that Iraq was not going to launch a second invasion.

ABC reported on August 3 that "U.S. intelligence sources today say that while Iraqi troops may be close to the border with Saudi Arabia, there is no indication that they're paused or in any position to mount an attack."[79] On August 4, ABC declared: "Iraqi troops have reportedly moved into a small neutral zone between Kuwait and Saudi Arabia," but noted: "the troops are setting up defensive positions, not preparing for an invasion."[80] On August 6, ABC assessed Iraq's options without mentioning the possibility that it might invade Saudi Arabia.

The news on August 7 sounded more ominous: "intelligence reports overnight indicated what the White House is calling an 'imminent threat to Saudi Arabia' from the very positioning of the Iraqi forces in Kuwait."[81] But this characterization of the threat to Saudi Arabia is telling in what is does *not* say: it does not offer any reason to believe that Iraq would attack. Jean Edward Smith quotes the president announcing the troop deployment on August 8:

> Iraq has massed an enormous war machine on the Saudi border, capable of initiating hostilities with little or no additional preparation. Given the Iraqi government's history of aggression against its own citizens as well as its neighbors, to assume that Iraq will not attack again would be unwise and unrealistic.[82]

As Smith observes, what is striking about this statement is that it offers no evidence that an Iraqi invasion of Saudi Arabia is coming; it simply

---

[77] Michael Ross, "U.S. Lawmakers Say Saudis Are Key to Action," *Los Angeles Times,* August 5, 1990, A8.
[78] *World News Tonight,* August 7, 1990.
[79] *World News Tonight,* August 3, 1990.
[80] *World News Tonight,* August 4, 1990.
[81] *World News Tonight,* August 7, 1990.
[82] Quoted in Smith, *George Bush's War,* p. 97.

notes Iraqi *capabilities*—which had been clear to U.S. officials from the outset—but omits the reassuring analysis of Iraqi *intentions* that had been offered up to this point. What had changed, it appears, was not the intentions or the behavior of the Iraqis, but the policy of the White House, creating the need for an Iraqi threat to Saudi Arabia to justify U.S. intervention.

Even this equivocal appeal to capabilities disappeared the next day, when a Defense Department spokesman told reporters that the Iraqi forces "seem to be in a defensive posture," and declared: "It would seem to us that they are working to hold onto what they have acquired."[83] As Smith observes, it is an odd notion that "a major army poised to sweep across the frontier one day should be dug in the next."[84] The 24-hour Iraqi threat to Saudi Arabia, in other words, appears to have been a White House creation.

In addition to intelligence reports indicating that Iraq would not attack Saudi Arabia, there were other reasons to question the premise that such a plan existed. Iraq had issued repeated threats to invade Kuwait before August 1 and had received mixed signals from the United States;[85] American signals on Saudi Arabia once Iraq entered Kuwait were crystal clear. Iraq had long-standing historical claims on Kuwait, but not on Saudi Arabia, and it harbored specific grievances against Kuwait regarding disputed oil reserves. As the *Washington Post* reported on August 4, U.S. officials had seen "signs indicating that Iraq was not preparing to attack Saudi Arabia: Iraqi propaganda organs have avoided any verbal attacks on the kingdom and had stated no border or oil pricing grievances against the Saudis as they had against Kuwait."[86] Hindsight is not required to see that the invasion of Kuwait did not mean an invasion of Saudi Arabia would be next, as those wielding the Hitler analogy claimed. If Democrats opposed to military intervention before August 7 changed their minds on the basis of an Iraqi threat to Saudi Arabia, they had been "persuaded by reasons that someone else, in different political circumstances, would not find persuasive."[87]

Even if the need to defend Saudi Arabia is stipulated, other options existed besides intervention on the ground. The Pentagon had a range of options for defending Saudi Arabia without the use of ground troops. On August 4, the *Washington Post* reported:

---

[83] "Defense Department Regular Briefing," *Federal News Service*, August 9, 1990.

[84] Smith, *George Bush's War*, p. 98.

[85] Ibid., pp. 41–62.

[86] Patrick E. Tyler, "U.S. Warns Iraq Not to Attack Saudi Arabia," *Washington Post*, August 4, 1990, A1.

[87] Zaller, "Strategic Politicians," pp. 254–55.

Pentagon leaders yesterday offered President Bush a list of military options for repelling a possible Iraqi invasion into Saudi Arabia that included U.S. air attacks against Iraqi military forces and critical targets inside Iraq, but did not recommend a major deployment of U.S. ground forces to the region, according to Pentagon officials.[88]

In fact, the *Washington Post* reported on August 4, *before* the White House had made its decision, "Military leaders have recommended against sending U.S. ground forces to the Mideast."[89] In preparing for "a possible Iraqi invasion into Saudi Arabia," it turns out, actors inside the Pentagon argued *against* the use of ground troops. Bob Woodward reports that even General Colin L. Powell, the chairman of the Joint Chiefs of Staff, was opposed to the idea of intervention on the ground in August.[90]

What if the White House had decided not to send troops to Saudi Arabia, and Iraq had then invaded? As we have seen, after the president's policy was announced the media framed the alternative to U.S. intervention on the ground as Iraqi domination of the Persian Gulf. But the Pentagon had other options. The August 4 edition of the *Washington Post* offers a review of the extraordinary number and scope of the options that existed for defending Saudi Arabia without ground troops:

In [the] event of an attack on Saudi Arabia, the United States could deploy F-15 and F-16 fighters from bases in Spain and West Germany, F-111 bombers from airstrips in England and F-14 fighter planes and A-6 bombers off the carrier USS Independence. . . .

In addition, the Strategic Air Command's B-52 long- range bomber force . . . could be deployed for a major operation. . . .

The United States also could launch and refuel aircraft out of Turkey and Israel, military official said. . . .

. . . Eight ships already are on station in the Persian Gulf. In addition, the carrier group led by the USS Eisenhower is plowing toward the eastern Mediterranean Sea. . . .

A third carrier group with the USS Saratoga and battleship USS Wisconsin is scheduled to leave Norfolk Monday, with a five-ship Marine amphibious group also deploying from the East Coast. . . .

The battleship, the Aegis guided-missile cruisers and the attack submarines accompanying the carrier groups will give the United States the added firepower potential of Tomahawk sea-launched cruise missiles.[91]

[88] Molly Moore, "Pentagon Provides Bush with List of Options for Defending Saudis," *Washington Post*, August 4, 1990, A17.
[89] Ibid.
[90] Bob Woodward, *The Commanders* (New York: Pocket Star Books, 1991), pp. 209–14.
[91] Moore, "Pentagon Provides Options."

This remarkable array of options, on the agenda in Washington until August 7—and no secret to the media—simply disappeared from public debate as an alternative to the use of ground troops once U.S. policy had been set.

It is also possible that the decision of the United Nations to endorse U.S. intervention and the troop contributions other nations made encouraged Democrats such as Hamilton, Nunn, Boren, and Cranston to change their position on the wisdom of a military response. But if international backing made military intervention easier to support, the president's extraordinary demonization of Saddam Hussein—to the point of seeming to preclude the option of a diplomatic resolution of the crisis—and his refusal to rule out a military offensive to free Kuwait, must have made U.S. intervention, with or without international support, appear even more dangerous than it had on August 1. Tucker and Hendrickson observe that Bush "used every opportunity to denounce Saddam Hussein in vitriolic and heated tones . . . in a way calculated to assault his pride," contrary to the "more measured diplomatic tone" that is generally used to conduct foreign affairs.[92] This was noted at the time: on August 7 the *Washington Post* reported "significant concern at high levels of the military that the growing confrontation with Saddam was not leaving him a face-saving 'out' from the crisis."[93] Inside the Pentagon, there were increasing fears that the president's demonization of the Iraqi leader might force a military confrontation.

New York Times columnist Tom Wicker, although not a critic of U.S. intervention, observed on August 9 that the official U.S. mission (and the one the Democrats supported) focused on the defense of Saudi Arabia. But the demand for the " 'immediate, unconditional and complete withdrawal of all Iraqi forces from Kuwait' and the restoration of the emirate . . . could only be a gamble on bringing about the downfall, not just the defeat, of Saddam Hussein." Wicker observed: "The President was careful neither to rule out nor to threaten 'pre-emptive strikes' . . . against Iraq itself. The inference surely must be taken, however, that if sanctions don't produce the desired results, military action is next."[94] It was clear at the outset, in other words, that the commitment Bush had made might well lead to a U.S. offensive to force Iraq out of Kuwait.

In sum, emerging grounds for supporting military intervention (the alleged Iraqi threat to Saudi Arabia and the backing of the United Na-

---

[92] Robert W. Tucker and David C. Hendrickson, *The Imperial Temptation: The New World Order and America's Purpose* (New York: Council on Foreign Relations Press, 1992), p. 96.

[93] Patrick E. Tyler, "U.N. Security Council Votes Embargo on Iraq," *Washington Post*, August 7, 1990, A1.

[94] Tom Wicker, "A New Kind of Crisis," *New York Times*, August 9, 1990, A23.

tions) must be weighed against emerging grounds for opposing it (the relentless demonization of Saddam Hussein and the refusal to rule out offensive action). It is possible that some of the Democrats who had argued against military intervention at the outset changed their minds on the basis of new information. But the balance of emerging information cannot be said to have made a change in the Democratic position inevitable. Good reason existed for journalistic curiosity about the mechanics of the formation of the Washington consensus in August 1990. Not once in the coverage I examined, however, does a reporter mention that leading Democrats and top Pentagon officials had not seen the need for U.S. intervention on the ground until the White House announced its decision.

The News in November

In November, when the Bush administration decided to double the number of American troops in Saudi Arabia and cancel their rotation—a de facto ultimatum to Iraq that it had to get out of Kuwait or be subject to military attack—Republicans were united in support of the president, and Democrats offered a range of opinions. The debate in November focused not on *whether* to use force, but *when* to use it: In the near future? Or not until sanctions had been tried and proven ineffective? As Entman and Page observe: "nearly all reported critics as well as supporters [of U.S. policy] agreed that *Iraq must be unconditionally dislodged from Kuwait by force, if necessary.* The arguments put forward by [critics of U.S. policy in Washington] did not contest the goal of dislodgement, or the means of force, but merely the question of immediate necessity."[95] The essence of the Democratic critique of U.S. policy in November is captured in a *New York Times* editorial, where the question is framed as: "What's the rush?"[96] Not found in this debate between the Republican "use force sooner" and Democratic "use force later" camps is a third position: do not use force, but instead either maintain sanctions indefinitely until Iraq withdraws from Kuwait, or find a diplomatic solution to the standoff. Narrow though it may have been, however, in November one does find a debate over U.S. policy in Washington.

In the *New York Times*, 7.9 percent of the paragraphs in the November case contained critical perspectives on U.S. policy not attributed to foreign sources (see table 4.1). This figure is five times greater than the figure for August, when just 1.6 percent of the paragraphs reported critical viewpoints. A front-page story on November 12 declared that a "national de-

---

[95] Entman and Page, "News before the Storm," p. 95, emphasis in original.
[96] "What's Wrong with the Siege?" *New York Times,* November 18, 1990, sec. 4, p. 16.

bate" had begun over "the question of whether the country's interests in the [Persian Gulf] region are worth defending in a war with Iraq."[97] A front-page story on November 13 reported opposition to the decision to increase the U.S. force in Saudi Arabia, and cited "critics who ask why the United States should not wait a year or more to see if economic sanctions force Iraq to withdraw from Kuwait."[98] A second article on November 13 reported Senator Nunn's view that Bush had made a "mistake" and had moved too fast toward war.[99] The next day, Senator Edward Kennedy appeared in a front-page story charging that Bush had set the United States on a "headlong course toward war."[100] A long article on November 15 examined the reaction of ordinary Americans, including a man who declared: "This is not World War II. This is like Vietnam. What you have is no declaration of war, and a chief executive hellbent on fighting. I can't understand why there isn't more outcry."[101] One article in 8 contained four or more critical paragraphs in November, in contrast to 1 article in 40 in August.

On ABC's *World News Tonight*, 6.1 percent of the paragraphs contained critical viewpoints not attributed to foreign sources, a figure over 10 times the 0.4 percent figure for August (see table 4.2). Two programs featured senators critical of Bush's policy. On November 11, ABC reported at the top of the news that "some members of Congress are already complaining the President has gone too far, too fast and too much on his own."[102] On November 12, the top story described "a growing number of politicians . . . who warned that President Bush is moving altogether too quickly toward war," including Senator Moynihan, who predicted: "We will leave the Gulf in ruins and we will have destroyed yet another presidency in the process."[103]

The rise and fall of critical coverage on *World News Tonight* between November 11 and November 14 shows how closely television news is indexed to debate in Washington. On November 11 and 12, leading Democrats in Congress questioned U.S. policy in the Gulf and declared that the president needed congressional authorization to launch a military offen-

---

[97] Michael Oreskes, "A Debate Unfolds over Going to War against the Iraqis," *New York Times,* November 12, 1990, A1.

[98] Michael R. Gordon, "When to Threaten Iraq?" *New York Times,* November 13, 1990, A1.

[99] Michael R. Gordon, "Nunn, Citing 'Rush' to War, Assails Decision to Drop Troop Rotation Plan," *New York Times,* November 12, 1990, A15.

[100] Andrew Rosenthal, "Senators Asking President to Call Session over Gulf," *New York Times,* November 14, 1990, A1.

[101] Elizabeth Kolbert, "No Talk of Glory, but of Blood on Sand," *New York Times,* November 15, 1990, A1.

[102] *World News Tonight,* November 11, 1990.

[103] *World News Tonight,* November 12, 1990.

sive. Some suggested that a special session of Congress might be needed to address the issue. On November 13 and 14, a temporary resolution emerged, as the Senate scheduled hearings on the Gulf crisis for the end of the month, and House Speaker Tom Foley and Senate majority leader George Mitchell declared themselves satisfied that the White House planned no military offensive in the immediate future, putting the idea of a special session on the back burner.

On November 11 and 12, opposition to U.S. policy in Washington was the top story on ABC. On November 13 and 14, the procedural issue of the congressional war powers dominated the domestic side of the coverage. When congressional leaders decided not to call a special session, however, the volume of critical coverage based on U.S. sources fell precipitously. As the Democratic leadership put its critique of U.S. policy on hold pending committee hearings, ABC shifted its focus to the international arena, as the Soviet Union and the NATO allies, for the moment, seemed to constitute the most immediate obstacle to the execution of the president's design.

The editorial decisions of American journalists often make perfect sense if one posits that the goal of journalism is to predict the future; therefore sources who are in the best position to affect the outcome of events are the ones reporters gravitate toward.[104] On November 11 and 12, the U.S. Congress appeared to be in such a position. When the possibility that Congress might seize control of U.S. policy subsided for a time on November 13 and 14, coverage of domestic opposition declined, and White House efforts to win international support for its policy moved to center stage on television news.

On the opinion pages of the *New York Times*, 10 of the 29 editorials and American-authored columns on the Gulf crisis in November were critical of U.S. policy (see table 4.3). Tom Wicker described the decision to double U.S. forces in the Gulf as "ill-considered"[105] and "unwanted."[106] James Reston and Senator Bill Bradley argued that sanctions needed more time.[107] In the one column that went beyond the framework of the use-force-now/use-force-later debate, Erwin Knoll, editor of the *Progressive* magazine, questioned the legitimacy of the state of Kuwait—with its "boundaries that were invented in the 1920s by the British Foreign Office"—and mentioned the failure of the United States to resist Chinese

[104] Entman and Page, "News before the Storm," pp. 93–94.
[105] Tom Wicker, "The More Things Change. . . ," *New York Times*, November 11, 1990, sec. 4, p. 17.
[106] Tom Wicker, "Bush's Midterm Crisis," *New York Times*, November 21, 1990, A23.
[107] James Reston, "Too Early for Bush to Dial 911," *New York Times*, November 13, 1990, A31; Bill Bradley, "Bush Has the Cards, So Why Bluff?" *New York Times*, November 15, 1990, A27.

aggression against Tibet or Indonesian aggression against East Timor.[108] But this is just 1 out of 29 opinion pieces. Page, in a detailed review of commentary on the Gulf crisis in the *New York Times* between November and January, concludes, "The viewpoints expressed . . . generally mirrored official debates." Few of the critical columns Page examined questioned the premise of Democrats in Congress that force might have to be used down the road if sanctions failed, and that a negotiated solution was out of the question.[109]

On the *MacNeil/Lehrer Newshour*, 10 of the 27 American guests (37 percent) in November were critical of U.S. policy (see table 4.4). Of special note here is that three of the guests expressed views that went beyond the critique Democrats in Congress had articulated. Edward Luttwak of the Center for Strategic and International Studies declared his opposition to "the whole ground force presence in the area."[110] Former State Department official George Ball suggested that some form of negotiation might be an option: "there is a formula that offers some possibilities for Saddam to save a little of his face."[111] Jesse Jackson noted that the U.S. had not used military power to enforce U.N. resolutions on Lebanon, the West Bank, or South Africa and questioned the need for military action to enforce the resolutions on Kuwait.[112]

The finding that three *MacNeil/Lehrer* guests stepped outside the terms of debate in Washington could be seen as evidence that conflict inside the government also opens up the news to critical perspectives that fall beyond the boundaries of Democratic-Republican debate. But these three guests constitute just one-ninth of those who appeared in this period, a figure that is not far out of line (although somewhat on the high side) with the percentage of guests speaking outside the spectrum of official debate in the Washington consensus cases.

Political Calculations in November

Why did Democrats back U.S. intervention in August but criticize it in November? The change in the nature of U.S. policy between August and November does not, in and of itself, explain the change in the Democratic reaction. It is true that in November the United States moved one step closer to going to war than it had moved in August. But the August deci-

---

[108] Erwin Knoll, "Why the Rush to War?" *New York Times,* November 8, 1990, A35.

[109] Benjamin I. Page, *Who Deliberates? Mass Media in Modern Democracy* (Chicago: University of Chicago Press, 1996), p. 36.

[110] *MacNeil/Lehrer Newshour,* November 9, 1990.

[111] *MacNeil/Lehrer Newshour,* November 13, 1990.

[112] *MacNeil/Lehrer Newshour,* November 12, 1990.

sion constituted a far more dramatic departure from existing policy than the November decision, creating a real possibility of war where none had existed before.

In August, journalists could see that in demanding an Iraqi withdrawal from Kuwait and comparing Saddam Hussein to Hitler, Bush had made it unlikely that U.S. troops would return home until there had been an unconditional Iraqi capitulation or a military offensive to force Iraq out of Kuwait. The *New York Times* noted that the president had "pledged as publicly and as forcefully as a President can do"[113] that Iraq's invasion of Kuwait would not stand, and reported that top administration officials had "made it clear that they were prepared to expand American military activity beyond the current 'defensive positions' in Saudi Arabia."[114] One official explained: " 'George Bush promised that this guy wouldn't end up with Kuwait. . . . He hasn't staked his life on that, but he may well have staked his political future on it. So in the end—six months, a year, who knows?—he may try anything.' "[115] The *Washington Post* too could read the writing on the wall: "U.S. officials believe that a long-term solution probably requires the removal from office of Saddam; for a man 'backed into a corner,' as Bush described the Iraqi leader Friday, that may leave no face-saving option but a bloody fight."[116] The official explanation of U.S. policy spoke of deterring an Iraqi invasion of Saudi Arabia, but the effective reduction of the alternatives in August to an Iraqi capitulation on Kuwait or a U.S. offensive to oust Iraq was clear to see.

Unless it is a law of politics that increasing the odds of war, on a scale of one to 10, from five to seven (what happened, at an approximation, in November) demands more criticism than increasing the odds of war from one to five (what happened in August), the change in the Democratic reaction requires an explanation. An essential element of the explanation is politics. In August, a Democratic party struggling to overcome a reputation for weakness on foreign policy would have criticized U.S. intervention at great political peril. Great efforts had been made in the 1980s to shed the Democratic image of weakness on foreign policy (see chapter 3), a project that opposition to U.S. intervention in the Persian Gulf could have undone. For this reason, I have argued, journalists should not have interpreted the failure of Democrats to speak out against U.S. intervention in August as justification for marginalizing critical perspectives outside of Washington.

[113] R. W. Apple Jr., "Iraq Proclaims Kuwait's Annexation; Bush Draws 'Line,' " *New York Times,* August 9, 1990, A1.

[114] Rosenthal, "U.S. Bets Troops," A14.

[115] Apple, "Iraq Proclaims Kuwait's Annexation."

[116] Rick Atkinson and David Hoffman, "Suddenly, a Long, Costly Crisis Looms," *Washington Post,* August 12, 1990, A1.

In November, Democrats could join the debate on *how* to use the forces stationed in the Saudi desert and question the decision to increase the size of the U.S. deployment, while still backing the use of the military to defend Saudi Arabia and to evict Iraq from Kuwait *if sanctions proved ineffective over time.* As Zaller observes: "no important Democratic spokesman urged Bush to withdraw American forces from the Gulf region, nor did any contend that Bush was wrong to send them there in the first place."[117] Most Democrats expressed support for the use of force against Iraq *at some future point*, if sanctions failed to get the job done. This reduced the political cost to the Democrats of criticizing the president's specific policy. (It should also be noted in this context that U.S. intervention in August fell two months before the 1990 elections; the November decision was announced just after the campaign season ended.)

Democrats had an additional reason to criticize the president in November that had not been a factor in August: the defense of the congressional war powers. In August, the war powers issue had been moot, as Bush had acted in response to a sudden and unexpected event. In November, however, Democrats in Congress either had to speak out on the war powers question or turn their backs on a constitutional principle their party had been fighting for decades to establish. And in arguing their case that the president needed congressional authorization to go to war, Democrats had to offer some commentary on the wisdom of his policy. To defend the congressional war powers in a forceful fashion, Democrats had to offer some kind of critique of U.S. policy itself. Otherwise their concern about Congress being consulted would have seemed pointless and irrelevant.

In resolving their uncertainly regarding what the United States should do about Iraq, Democrats had powerful political incentives to back the president in August. But in November the political logic of the situation was less restrictive. The argument is not that political calculations were decisive in the change in the Democratic position between August and November; it is that political calculations, which had in effect *ruled out* a critical Democratic response in August, made a critical response possible in November. Between August and November, the political logic of the situation had changed. And because of the indexing rule, the American public therefore received critical analysis of U.S. policy in the news in November, where there had been—except at the margins—no critical analysis of U.S. policy in August.

In sum, media coverage of U.S. intervention in the Persian Gulf in August and November 1990 supports the prediction of the indexing hypothesis. In November, with Democrats in Washington speaking out against U.S. policy, critical perspectives were easy to find in the news. In August,

[117] Zaller, "Elite Leadership of Opinion," pp. 196–97.

with a bipartisan consensus in Washington backing U.S. intervention, critical perspectives were marginalized in the media. Journalists questioned whether the president could *execute* his policy and achieve his own objectives in August, but declined to question the wisdom and justification of U.S. policy itself.

Critical perspectives on U.S. policy could have been reported in August if journalists had interviewed foreign-policy experts outside of Washington and interested, engaged citizens. Even Democrats in Washington questioned the need for military intervention in August before the president announced his decision. Once the policy had been set, however, Democratic critics fell silent, as it made no political sense for Democrats to speak out against a Republican military action, whatever their views on its merits might have been. In November, the political logic of the situation was less restrictive, and Democrats were in a better position to criticize the president's policy. Because of the indexing rule, the political calculations of the Democratic Party set the spectrum of debate in the news.

Five

The Rule and Some Exceptions

THE INDEXING of the spectrum of debate in the news to the spectrum of debate in Washington is a general pattern in American journalism; it is not a universal rule. When the figures for the eight cases examined in the content analysis are assembled in one table, the evidence in support of the indexing hypothesis is impressive (see table 5.1).

In the news section of the *New York Times*, on average 10.1 percent of the paragraphs in the Washington conflict cases were coded as critical; for the Washington consensus cases the figure is just 2.0 percent. One paragraph in 10 is critical in the Washington conflict cases, as opposed to 1 paragraph in 50 in the Washington consensus cases. On *World News Tonight*, the average for the Washington conflict cases is 8.9 percent (1 paragraph in 11); for the Washington consensus cases the figure is 1.5 percent (1 paragraph in 67). For the *New York Times*, the indexing effect is a factor of five; for *World News Tonight* it is a factor of six. (See the appendix for an expanded presentation of the findings.)

On the opinion pages of the *New York Times* and on the *MacNeil/Lehrer Newshour*, the aggregate figures show a strong, although less dramatic, indexing effect. On the opinion pages of the *Times*, on average 46 percent of the editorials and columns were critical in the Washington conflict cases; the figure is 14 percent in the Washington consensus cases. On the *MacNeil/Lehrer Newshour*, 34 percent of the guests were critical of U.S. intervention in the Washington conflict cases; the figure is 11 percent in the Washington consensus cases. For the opinion pages and the *Newshour* the indexing effect is about a factor of three.

It might seem natural for the indexing effect to be greater in the news section and on *World News Tonight*, where the focus is on reporting unfolding events, than on the opinion pages and *MacNeil/Lehrer*, which are designed to offer analysis and commentary. But it is not clear that this is the best interpretation of the evidence. On *MacNeil/Lehrer*, the figure for one Washington consensus case—Libya (35 percent)—greatly exceeds the figures for the other three. In the *New York Times* too, the figure for Libya (29 percent) is much higher than the figures for the other Washington consensus cases. If Libya is excluded from the calculation, the average rate of critical editorials and columns in the *New York Times* for the other three Washington consensus cases is 9 percent, against 46 percent for the

TABLE 5.1

Critical Paragraphs, Guests, and Editorials and Columns, Washington Conflict versus Washington Consensus

	New York Times News Section	ABC News	MacNeil/ Lehrer	New York Times Opinion Pages
Washington Conflict				
Grenada	8.3	9.0	39	44
Gulf War (November)	7.9	6.1	37	34
Somalia	16.9	10.7	39	67
Haiti	7.1	9.6	22	39
Average	10.1	8.9	34	46
Washington Consensus				
Libya	1.6	1.8	35	29
Panama	1.6	1.5	0	13
Gulf War (August)	1.6	0.4	6	3
Gulf War (January)	3.2	2.4	4	12
Average	2.0	1.5	11	14
Not Counting Libya	2.1	1.4	3	9

Note: Figures are percentages

Washington conflict cases; on *MacNeil/Lehrer*, if Libya is excluded the average for the Washington consensus cases is 3 percent, against 34 percent for the Washington conflict cases. If the Libya case is excluded, the indexing effect on the *Times* opinion pages is a factor of 5; on *MacNeil/ Lehrer* it is a factor of 10 (see table 5.1).

This chapter first examines why the Libya case does not match the other Washington consensus cases on the *New York Times* opinion pages and *MacNeil/Lehrer*. It then investigates why the figures for the Gulf War (January) case in the *New York Times* news section and on *World News Tonight* exceed those for the other Washington consensus cases, and why the figures for Somalia in the *New York Times* exceed those for the other Washington conflict cases. The chapter concludes with some observations about the case of Haiti.

Libya and the Impact of NATO Opposition

In January 1986, after a series of terrorist incidents that appeared to be tied to Libya, "the Reagan administration set in motion an active policy that would utilize coherent and escalating political, economic, and military pressures in an attempt to achieve the declared objective of ending

[Libyan leader] Qaddafi's sponsorship of international terrorism."[1] Washington "imposed a total ban on direct import and export trade with Libya."[2] The European allies, however, declined to join in this strategy of economic and diplomatic isolation.[3] The Reagan administration then commenced a series of military exercises off the coast of Libya. In March, U.S. and Libyan fighter planes clashed after U.S. warships entered international waters that Libya claimed as its own.[4] Although some in the administration viewed the incident as justification for an attack on Libya, no Americans had been killed, and "consequently, the plan for a full attack on Libyan targets was not implemented" at this time.[5]

Finally, after U.S. intelligence concluded that Libya had been behind a terrorist attack in West Berlin on April 5 that killed 2 Americans and injured 70, U.S. planes struck a number of military targets in Libya, including a command center located near the Gadhafi family residence. In addition to the military targets hit, the raid struck buildings in a residential area (including the French embassy) and killed a few dozen civilians.[6] The bombing, which the White House described as an act of retaliation and a show of American resolve, presumably achieved these objectives, although it failed to secure the unstated objective of ending Gadhafi's rule.

As in the Panama, Gulf War (August), and Gulf War (January) cases, U.S. intervention in Libya won bipartisan support in Washington. *Congressional Quarterly* reported "overwhelming support" for the raid: "In both political parties and nearly across the political spectrum, there was general agreement . . . that the U.S. air strike was justified."[7]

Coded as critical in the Libya case were paragraphs expressing or indicating opposition to the use of force or questioning its justification. As in the other cases, paragraphs questioning the *execution* of U.S. policy on tactical or procedural grounds were not coded as critical, unless the wisdom or justification of U.S. intervention itself was questioned.[8] In the *New York Times* news section, just 1 paragraph in 63 on Libya contained

[1] Tim Zimmermann, "Coercive Diplomacy and Libya," in *The Limits of Coercive Diplomacy*, ed. Alexander L. George and William E. Simons (Boulder, Colo.: Westview Press, 1994), p. 202.
[2] Ibid., p. 207.
[3] Ibid., p. 208.
[4] Ibid., pp. 211–12.
[5] Ibid., p. 212.
[6] Ibid., pp. 213–15.
[7] Pat Towell, "After Raid on Libya, New Questions on Hill," *Congressional Quarterly Weekly Report* 44, April 19, 1986, pp. 838–39.
[8] Paragraphs simply suggesting that the U.S. raid would not reduce the threat of terrorism were not coded as critical (unless criticism of the bombing is otherwise indicated), as the Reagan administration itself had not made this claim, offering instead "retaliation" as the reason for the bombing.

a critical viewpoint on U.S. policy not attributed to a foreign source, a figure comparable to the other Washington consensus cases. The figure for *World News Tonight* is similar: 1 paragraph in 56.

On the opinion pages of the *New York Times* and on *MacNeil/Lehrer*, however, the figures for Libya diverge from the other Washington consensus cases. Against the 6 percent of U.S. guests on *MacNeil/Lehrer* who offered critical viewpoints on the decision to send American troops to Saudi Arabia in August 1990, 4 percent in the Gulf War (January) case, and zero in the Panama case, 35 percent of the American guests in the Libya case expressed criticism of U.S. policy. On the opinion pages of the *New York Times*, the figures are 3 percent for the Gulf War (August), 12 percent for the Gulf War (January), 13 percent for Panama, and 29 percent for Libya. Libya, in other words, looks like a Washington consensus case in the news section, but a Washington conflict case on the opinion pages. An explanation is needed.

Although a consensus in Washington supported the attack on Libya, the European allies—except for Britain—registered strong opposition. This opposition, moreover, manifested itself in a way that could not be ignored in the United States. A column in the *Los Angeles Times* explains:

> When President Reagan appeared on television Monday night to explain the Libyan strike to the American people, he was as effective as ever.
>
> But for once he was upstaged—by a line. For by far the most dramatic thing about the Administration's presentation was the map used by Secretary of Defense Caspar W. Weinberger to show the route taken by the F-111s on their flight from England to Tripoli and Benghazi. The line went around Brittany, the Bay of Biscay, and the Iberian Peninsula, through the Straits of Gibraltar and across the Mediterranean. Nowhere between England and Libya did it touch land, though most of the land involved was that of America's NATO allies. . . .
>
> The etching of this line on the mind of the American people is likely to be the most enduring and important consequence of the Libyan episode. . . . It shows, in the most graphic way possible, how the United States' allies—other than Great Britain—view the North Atlantic Treaty Organization.[9]

It is not just that France and others in NATO opposed the American attack on Libya. In declining to let U.S. planes based in Britain use French airspace on route to Libya, France made its opposition to American policy *tangible*, dramatically reinforcing its description of the raid as "an action of reprisals which itself re-launches the chain of violence."[10]

---

[9] Owen Harries, "The Line of Shame," *Los Angeles Times,* April 17, 1986, pt. 2, p. 7.

[10] "U.S. Hits Libya to End 'Terror,' but Move Criticized by Allies," Reuters, April 15, 1986. Zimmermann reports that "French denial of overflight rights, . . . doubled the F-111 flying times, reduced the bomb loads each plane could carry, and reduced to six (from eigh-

With the exception of Britain, one finds the same reaction throughout Europe. The Italian prime minister described the bombing as "a decision which does not take due account of the value of the Euro-American partnership" and argued that "far from weakening international terrorism . . . such military actions run the risk of provoking a further explosion of fanaticism, extremism, criminal and suicide actions."[11] The West German government offered the view that "force is not a very promising way of dealing with things" and expressed a preference for international dialogue.[12] The Dutch government announced that it deplored the attack on Libya, and others in NATO made similar declarations.[13]

The division in NATO emerged as a major story. The *Los Angeles Times* declared: "The U.S. raid on Libya created a tense and troublesome split Tuesday between the United States and most of its allies, pushing the United States more out of step with Europe than at any time since the war in Vietnam."[14] Reuters warned of "a potentially severe crisis" in NATO and reported that some had "compared it to serious transatlantic rifts over the 1979–81 U.S.-Iranian hostage crisis and the Soviet military intervention in Afghanistan."[15] An editorial in the *New York Times* asserted that "the failure to cooperate against Libya plants poisonous seeds of disintegration" within the Western alliance.[16]

The point, in sum, is not just that foreign governments opposed American policy; it is that *the NATO allies* opposed American policy, indicating division in the alliance that was the cornerstone of U.S. foreign policy and the Cold War order in Europe. This opposition, moreover, manifested itself not just in the statements European governments issued, but in a tangible action that affected the execution of the operation, graphically illustrated in the line on the Pentagon's map.[17] European opposition to the bombing therefore generated great interest in the United States.

I have argued that criticism of U.S. foreign policy from the Soviet Union and other official enemies, or from Latin America or the Middle East (Israel is an exception), does not have much impact in the United

---

teen) the number of F-111s that could hit each target selected" ("Coercive Diplomacy," pp. 219–20).

[11] Barry Moody, "Italy Strongly Attacks U.S. Raid," Reuters, April 15, 1986.

[12] Paul Holmes, "Kohl Expresses Sympathy but Not Support for U.S. Raid," Reuters, April 15, 1986.

[13] "U.S. Hits Libya."

[14] Stanley Meisler, "U.S.-Europe Split Worst since Vietnam," *Los Angeles Times,* April 16, 1986, p. 1.

[15] Paul Taylor, "Transatlantic Crisis Looms over U.S. Raid on Libya," Reuters, April 15, 1986.

[16] "What Are Allies For?" *New York Times,* April 17, 1986, A30.

[17] This point is made in W. Lance Bennett, "An Introduction to Journalism Norms and Representations of Politics," *Political Communication* 13 (October–December 1996): 378.

States. I have not, however, addressed the question of the NATO allies. The decision to ignore European criticism is inconsequential in the other three Washington consensus cases, as critical perspectives attributed to European sources in the *New York Times* news section do not have a significant impact contrary to the pattern of U.S. sources.[18] Libya is the one intervention that won bipartisan support in the United States but generated strong opposition in Europe, and this opposition received substantial coverage. In contrast to the 1.6 percent of *New York Times* paragraphs reporting critical American viewpoints on the bombing of Libya, 8.7 percent reported European opposition to U.S. policy. A similar pattern is evident on *World News Tonight*.

European criticism is a significant aspect of the Libya coverage.[19] Although European opposition seems to have had no impact on the spectrum of *American* debate in the news section of the *New York Times* and on *World News Tonight*, the opinion pages of the *Times* and *MacNeil/Lehrer* tell a different story. Five of the seven critical columns in the *Times* offer opposition to U.S. policy inside NATO as a principle reason for questioning it. James Reston observes that "some of the allies, especially the French, are disturbed by charges that they are being 'soft' on Colonel Qaddafi and indifferent to the threat of terrorism" and explains their objections to the bombing.[20] Flora Lewis quotes a Labour Party official in Britain who compares U.S. policy to "a comic-strip. . . , Rambo out to zap the baddies," and she urges Washington to act "in concert with friends" instead of "provoking them to take stands against America's display of anger and frustration."[21] A second Reston column observes: "At no time in recent memory has the U.S. been condemned by informed opinion across the world as it has been for this bombing."[22] Two more critical columns focus on European opposition to the raid.[23]

It is clear that the authors of these columns were concerned about European opposition to the military strike. *New York Times* columnists, who in the other cases offered opinions that fell inside the boundaries of debate in Washington, seem in the Libya case to have been influenced by reaction

---

[18] Critical perspectives attributed to European sources were found in 0.3 percent of the paragraphs in the Panama case, 0.1 percent in the Gulf War (August) case, and 1.1 percent in the Gulf War (January) case.

[19] On this point see Scott L. Althaus et al., "Revising the Indexing Hypothesis: Officials, Media, and the Libya Crisis," *Political Communication* 13 (October–December 1996): 407–21.

[20] James Reston, "Unanswered Questions," *New York Times,* April 16, 1986, A27.

[21] Flora Lewis, "The Concern Is Results," *New York Times,* April 17, 1986, A31.

[22] James Reston, "Leave It to the People?" *New York Times,* April 20, 1986, sec. 4, p. 25.

[23] Anthony Lewis, "Reasons for Doubt," *New York Times,* April 21, 1986, A19; Flora Lewis, "What Is an Ally?" *New York Times,* April 27, 1986, sec. 4, p. 23.

in the NATO capitals. Other foreign sources are no match for the European allies in terms of credibility to this set of commentators. Latin American governments opposed the invasion of Panama, but this made no great impression on the op-ed page. Figures in the Middle East opposed to U.S. intervention in the Persian Gulf failed to get the attention of *New York Times* columnists. But European opposition does seem to explain the unexpected percentage of critical columns in the *Times* in the Libya case. In the one case in which there is a departure from the indexing rule on the opinion pages, an explanation is found not in the impact of nonofficial sources in the United States, but in the reaction of the governments of the NATO allies.

The six critical guests on *MacNeil/Lehrer* do not explicitly address European opposition to the bombing, but they offer the same argument against U.S. policy the Europeans had made. The Europeans claimed that military action could be expected to inspire *more* terrorism and to *strengthen* Gadhafi's hold on power in Libya. On the *Newshour*, a former State Department official, a journalist, a professor, two former Middle East hostages, and the sister of a third hostage made precisely this point. In the representative words of former hostage Benjamin Weir: "I think the attempt to try to liquidate terrorists by military action is really quite futile."[24] Although I am unable to prove that it had a decisive impact, the expression of this critique of U.S. policy in Paris, Bonn, Rome, and other NATO capitals must have made it appear more legitimate to the producers of the *Newshour*, who put on the program four outside-Washington American guests who offered this perspective.

Of the six critical guests, three appeared in a segment that presented the perspective of American hostages in the Middle East, whose well-being seemed to have been put in jeopardy by the military strike.[25] Two former Middle East hostages and the sister of a third argued for a diplomatic response to terrorism. It might seem inevitable that the *Newshour* would explore this aspect of the story. But hostages played a major part in the Gulf War (August) and Panama cases too. U.S. intervention in Saudi Arabia inspired Iraq to seize *thousands* of hostages, including Americans.[26] U.S. intervention in Panama—justified, like the Libya raid, as a response to violence against Americans—inspired the seizure of several American hostages, three of whom were killed.[27] In each case there is a hostage angle to report. But it is only when the NATO allies made the point that U.S.

[24] *MacNeil/Lehrer Newshour,* April 18, 1986.
[25] Ibid.
[26] Clifford Krauss, "Baghdad Seals Off the Exit of Foreigners across Border," *New York Times,* August 10, 1990, A1.
[27] Buckley, *Panama,* p. 241.

policy threatened the well-being of Western hostages—an argument that had just as much force in the other cases—that this angle is examined on the *Newshour.*

The evidence of a single case is not enough to support general conclusions about the impact of European criticism on media coverage of U.S. foreign policy.[28] If one rejects the argument that Libya is a special case because of the reaction of the NATO allies, the aggregate figures show an indexing effect of a factor of three on the opinion pages of the *New York Times* and on *MacNeil/Lehrer.* If the argument just made has force, however, and the case of Libya is excluded on the ground that it falls into a third category (Washington consensus/NATO conflict) that was not included in the research design, the indexing effect is much stronger: a factor of 5 in the *New York Times,* a factor of 10 on the *MacNeil/Lehrer Newshour.* As it is not possible to establish that one interpretation is correct on the basis of a single case, table 5.1 averages the figures for the Washington consensus cases with and without Libya. My own conclusion is that NATO's opposition does explain the unexpected findings on Libya, and that Libya should therefore be understood as a special case.

The Gulf War and Antiwar Demonstrations

A second case that deviates from the pattern of the others in a direction contrary to the indexing hypothesis—although much less dramatically—is the Gulf War (January) case. *Congressional Quarterly* writes: "Congress rushed to support President Bush after he sent U.S. forces into battle against Iraq."[29] In the news section of the *New York Times,* however, the percentage of critical paragraphs in the Gulf War case—3.2 percent—is double the figure of 1.6 percent for the other three Washington consensus cases (see table 5.1). *World News Tonight* also contains more critical paragraphs in the Gulf War case. On the opinion pages of the *Times* and on the *MacNeil/Lehrer Newshour* the Gulf War case fits the pattern of the others (except Libya), but in the news section and on the evening news it does not.

[28] Althaus et. al. ("Revising the Indexing Hypothesis") conclude from the coverage of U.S. policy toward Libya in 1986 that the indexing hypothesis needs to be revised to include foreign elites. I believe this would be an overgeneralization based on one case, as the NATO allies are unique in their credibility to elite commentators on U.S. foreign policy, and the Libya case is unique in the extent to which European opposition to U.S. policy manifested itself in a tangible form—the French denial of airspace—that made it a central element of the story.

[29] Carroll J. Doherty, "Congress Applauds President from Sidelines of War," *Congressional Quarterly Weekly Report* 49, January 19, 1991, p. 176.

TABLE 5.2
Impact of Demonstration Stories on Washington Consensus
Cases in *New York Times*

	Critical Paragraphs (%)	*Not Counting Demonstration Stories (%)*
Libya	1.6	1.6
Panama	1.6	1.0
Gulf War (August)	1.6	1.6
Gulf War (January)	3.2	1.7

The Gulf War is the one military action in this study that inspired major mass demonstrations against American policy in the United States. U.S. intervention in Grenada, Panama, and Libya sparked small protests here and there, but the Gulf War produced sizable demonstrations in Washington. In contrast to criticism expressed in the NATO capitals, one does not expect mass demonstrations against American foreign policy to have much influence on elite commentators, unless there is evidence of a general deterioration of public support. One does, however, expect demonstrations to be reported in the news section and on the evening news.

The potential for an antiwar movement had been a matter of some interest in the media during the buildup to the Gulf War. When the war started, most observers expected it to be a greater struggle than it turned out to be. While polls showed strong support for the war, U.S. intervention in Vietnam also had strong support at the beginning, before the casualties started to mount. History therefore suggested that domestic opposition might emerge as an obstacle to the war effort.

In the *New York Times*, 182 paragraphs out of 5,688 (3.2 percent) report criticism of the decision to go to war or questions about its justification not attributed to foreign sources. Of those paragraphs, 80 are about antiwar demonstrations. If those 80 paragraphs are excluded, the figure of 3.2 percent falls to 1.7 percent. If coverage of protest activities is factored out of the Libya, Panama, and Gulf War (August) cases too, the figure for the Gulf War (January) case no longer stands out (see table 5.2). Coverage of mass demonstrations appears to be the unique aspect of this case.

Media coverage of mass demonstrations against the Gulf War offered an avenue for critical perspectives to get into the news. But the *New York Times* often used sources in the crowd—instead of organizers or speakers— to frame stories that subverted the message of the demonstration. A story on January 18 on the response of ordinary Americans to the Gulf War, for example, observes, "Some who protested on Wednesday night thought the better of it yesterday." One protester explains: "When the bombing started, I felt the electricity and nostalgia of opposing a war. . . . But today it hit me: this is a real war out there. People will die. I'm older than I was in the Vietnam War. There was a momentary exhilaration Wednesday, but nostalgia is short lived."[30] Although antiwar activities are mentioned, this wavering critic is the sole protester to speak in the story.

The first story in the *New York Times* to focus on antiwar demonstrations appeared under the headline: "A War Again Stirs Anguish, but of a Quieter Kind."[31] The theme here is not the fact—as reported in the article—that "campuses have come alive with protests" against (and demonstrations in support of) the war, but the "Anguish" of students "born in the shadow of the defiant 1960s . . . struggling to reconcile their feelings about the conflict in the Persian Gulf with expectations of how they ought to act." The implication that student protests are based not on genuine opposition to the Gulf War, but on a desire to imitate the behavior of students in the 1960s, is repeated in the third and fourth paragraphs, which state that students "feel the pressure of . . . living up to the legacy of a previous generation of antiwar protesters," and see the war as a chance to prove that they are not "conservative and apathetic."

What is striking is that the article offers no evidence to support this theory of the motivation of the students. On the contrary, a student at Kent State University asserts that "people are not being actively against the war in the name of what happened on May 4 [1970]. They see something in Iraq that they don't believe in." The students who appear in this story do not seem to have Vietnam on their minds, although the reporter evidently does. A second student who mentions Vietnam does so to argue *for* the Gulf War: "If we don't support [the war], it will be Vietnam all over again." Based on the evidence in the article itself, a better frame would be that some students are opposed to the war, but *not* those who are thinking about Vietnam.

A second protest story is constructed in the same fashion: the headline and opening paragraphs in opposition to the evidence in the rest of the article. "News from Front Blunts Protests"[32] reports a demonstration in Washington that police estimated at 25,000 people (organizers claimed 100,000) and quotes some of those opposed to the war: an antiwar organizer who compares the war on television to a video game that denies the

[30] Jane Gross, "Anxious Nation, Drawn Together for Support, Exhibits a Quiet Pride," *New York Times,* January 18, 1991, A14.

[31] Anthony DePalma, "A War Again Stirs Anguish, but of a Quieter Kind," *New York Times,* January 20, 1991, p. 18.

[32] Peter Applebome, "News from Front Blunts Protests," *New York Times,* January 21, 1991, A12.

reality of "bodies being torn apart"; a woman who feels the war is "deflecting all our energy away from problems at home"; and a peace activist who argues that soldiers did not join the military "to fight a war for oil profits." Yet the article begins with a demonstrator who *supports* the war:

> Before the bombs began falling over Baghdad, David Pierce was a staunch opponent of military action in the Middle East. Now he feels that the United States has no choice but to keep fighting.
>
> "A lot of people who were against fighting the war have switched sides," said Mr. Pierce. . . . Despite his doubts, he came with his wife and two children to Saturday's antiwar demonstration near the White House.
>
> Mr. Pierce said he went to clarify his own thinking and to show moral concern. "Things aren't as clear-cut to me anymore," he said, "but I just think now that we've started fighting, we have to stay the course."

Thus does an article about a major antiwar demonstration begin with a man who renounces his opposition to the war. This is an interesting phenomenon, of course, but Mr. Pierce surely represents a small minority of those in attendance. The frame is also odd in view of a paragraph deep in the article that observes: "the [antiwar] movement has already seen local protests, participation from veterans and families of servicemen and mainstream support in a way rarely seen in the Vietnam protests," contradicting the suggestion that the antiwar movement had faltered in its conviction.

Why does an article about a national antiwar demonstration in Washington and local protests that are said to have mobilized "cotton mill workers, farmers, truck drivers and other workers" in North Carolina, lead with the uncertain Mr. Pierce? There is no reason to postulate a prowar bias at the *New York Times*. When there is consensus in Washington, journalists focus not on the wisdom or justification of U.S. policy, but on the ability of the president to execute it. Going into the Gulf War with Vietnam looming in American memory, there was concern that the public might not support a major military engagement. It is in this context that reporters examined the antiwar movement in search of news. Could domestic opposition have an impact on the efforts of the White House to prosecute the war?

If this is the question, and the polls indicate support for the war in the mass public, then the news peg the story of this demonstration hangs on is that the antiwar movement is *not* going to affect the war effort. One might question the judgment that 25,000 is an unimpressive turnout for a protest against a war that had just started and had produced few American casualties; the tens of thousands who marched in Washington could have been judged an impressive beginning for the movement. (Where were the protests against the Vietnam War at such an early stage?) But the question American journalists posed was not: "Is there an antiwar movement, who supports it, and why?" but instead: "Does this affect the war effort?" For the time being it clearly did not, and the framing of the story reflected this assessment.

The other major protest story in the *New York Times* reported a second demonstration in Washington the next weekend officially estimated at 75,000 people (organizers claimed 250,000).[33] This article, "Day of Protests Is the Biggest Yet," does not subvert the message of the demonstrators. As the headline indicates, the standard this second demonstration is measured against is not the protests of the Vietnam era, but the first Gulf War protest.

The third and fourth paragraphs report that the antiwar movement had adjusted its tactics in an effort to win more support:

> Unlike last week's antiwar march here, which was dominated by left-leaning groups and drew about 25,000 people, today's demonstration, . . . conducted amid a blizzard of American flags, seemed intent on conveying a mainstream message that Americans can best support their troops by stopping a war that is not in the nation's interest.
>
> "We learned a lot of things from Vietnam," said Joe Miller, a Vietnam veteran. . . . "One thing is that we have to separate the warriors from the war and that you don't blame the troops for the policy they're carrying out. I support the troops by wanting them home alive."[34]

In contrast to the first demonstration, where the news was that it had not measured up to the protests of the 1960s and would have no bearing on U.S. policy, the story of the second demonstration was that support for the antiwar movement appeared to be increasing, as its strategy and tactics improved. Sensing an upsurge in the potential impact of the antiwar movement, the *New York Times* reported the second demonstration in more positive terms.

ABC's Gulf War coverage also contains more critical perspectives than the other Washington consensus cases. As in the *New York Times*, coverage of antiwar demonstrations is the explanation. Of the 47 paragraphs coded as critical, 28 reported antiwar protests. If protest stories are excluded, the figure of 2.4 percent falls to 0.9 percent. The figures for the Libya, Panama, and Gulf War (August) cases, if protest stories are excluded, are 1.8 percent, 0.7 percent, and 0.4 percent.

As in the *New York Times*, two of ABC's four protest stories are framed in terms that undermine the oppositional message of the demonstrators.

[33] Elsa Walsh and Paul Valentine, "War Protest Draws Tens of Thousands Here," *Washington Post,* January 27, 1991, A1.

[34] Peter Applebome, "Day of Protests Is the Biggest Yet," *New York Times,* January 27, 1991, p. 17.

A story from Kent State University begins: "Once again at Kent State, students are demonstrating about U.S. involvement in a faraway war, but this time the loudest chants support American policy." The story is about prowar sentiment at Kent State; just one student speaks in opposition to the war. The dramatic structure of this story is simple: in the 1960s students opposed war; in the 1990s students support war, and the few opponents are on the defensive.[35]

A story from Arcata, California, also focuses on support for the war. The Arcata City Council had declared the city a sanctuary zone for war resisters, and "thousands of other residents were furious." At a meeting attended by over a thousand people, the city council rescinded the order and apologized. One man declared: "No retraction of this resolution can de-expose the true colors of this council," which in his view were "not red, white and blue," but "a solid pink."[36] Four opponents of the antiwar resolution are quoted, and two supporters. The point here is not to criticize ABC, as the coverage may have reflected the balance of opinion at Kent State and in Arcata. It is that much of the criticism of the war on ABC is reported inside a prowar frame.

ABC also covered the demonstrations in Washington. In neither story does a speaker or organizer appear. As in the *New York Times*, the story on the second demonstration is more positive, concluding: "Whatever the number [in attendance], it was an enormous protest against the war only ten days old." Neither story contains substantive criticism of U.S. policy, a *reason* to oppose the war, although the stories do indicate the existence of opposition in the United States.

Although antiwar demonstrations caused the *New York Times* news section and ABC to report the reaction of some ordinary citizens, critical foreign-policy *experts* were essentially invisible in their Gulf War coverage. Of the sources to which critical paragraphs in the *New York Times* were attributed in January, 60 percent (109) were ordinary people; just 3 percent (5) were foreign-policy experts.[37] It is clear from the debate leading up to the war that a substantial number of foreign-policy experts outside of Washington opposed it, and it is hard to imagine that the experts simply switched sides once the war started, as the 42 percent of the House of Representatives and 47 percent of the Senate who had voted not to authorize war in January seem to have done.[38] Yet except at the margins, the

---

[35] *World News Tonight,* January 24, 1991.

[36] Ibid.

[37] The other critical sources were religious figures (27), politicians (25), and public-interest organizations (16). Public-interest organizations received coverage because of their participation in antiwar demonstrations.

[38] Smith, *George Bush's War,* p. 248.

New York Times declined to include critical foreign-policy experts in its Gulf War coverage.

On ABC, not one foreign-policy expert expressed criticism of the war, nor does one find a representative of a public-interest organization. Instead, ABC consulted the "person-on-the-street." Some of these people offered simple declarations of opposition, such as "It's senseless," or "I'm very much against the war," but just 3 paragraphs of ABC News transcript—out of 1,940—offer an *argument* against U.S. policy, a *reason* to oppose the war. The attribution of criticism of U.S. policy to random ordinary people who offer no reason for their position creates the impression that the experts—the politicians, the generals, the retired diplomats—support the war, while certain ordinary people, for reasons that are not quite made clear, do not.

On the *MacNeil/Lehrer Newshour*, just 2 out of 46 American guests were critical of the decision to go to war.[39] Zbigniew Brzezinski mentioned to Jim Lehrer near the end of an interview: "I felt and I still do feel that this issue wasn't so urgent as to require an immediate or early military response. . . . Iraq wasn't all that powerful. . . . It really is a third world country."[40] Representative Patricia Schroeder made the same point, describing Iraq as "a paper tiger," and arguing that economic sanctions could have worked.[41] Notwithstanding the national debate that had just been held, noncritical Americans on the program outweighed critics 96 percent to 4 percent. As actors in Washington united behind the war, the *Newshour* joined in the official consensus.

The *New York Times* published 58 American-authored editorials and op-eds on the Gulf War during the January period. Seven (12 percent) expressed opposition to U.S. policy. Anna Quindlen argued that Kuwait was not worth American lives and that the U.S. should not be the world's policeman.[42] Tom Wicker offered a number of objections to the war, such as the diversion of resources from domestic needs, and criticized Bush for demanding "Iraq's unconditional withdrawal from Kuwait—the equivalent of unconditional surrender—as the sole test of whether there would be war."[43] Two columns by Anthony Lewis criticized the war, one arguing that "President Bush would have been wiser to let sanctions continue working rather than plunge into war,"[44] the other holding that in his ob-

[39] I could not get access to the January 21 and January 23 editions of the *Newshour;* the figures cited therefore do not include guests on those dates.

[40] *MacNeil/Lehrer Newshour,* January 17, 1991.

[41] *MacNeil/Lehrer Newshour,* January 18, 1991.

[42] Anna Quindlen, "Personally," *New York Times,* January 17, 1991, A23.

[43] Tom Wicker, "The War on the Tube," *New York Times,* January 23, 1991, A19.

[44] But Lewis goes on to argue: "now that we are in it, to pull back would be far worse than pressing the war to the quickest possible end." He concludes that "It is a just war—if

session with Iraq and Kuwait, Bush had compromised the U.S. effort to handle a crisis of greater significance: the Soviet crackdown in Lithuania.[45] Three more columns were critical of the war.

Seven critical columns is not an insignificant number, but it pales next to the 51 columns that were not critical. Even in the case of a war that the *New York Times* editorial page, 42 percent of the House, and 47 percent of the Senate had opposed just before it started, noncritical editorials and op-eds outnumber critical ones 88 percent to 12 percent.

There are two ways to interpret this finding. On the one hand, in the Gulf War case, unlike the cases of Libya, Panama, and the August intervention in Saudi Arabia, a debate had been conducted in Washington, and the prowar side had prevailed. As the pros and cons of military action had been debated before the decision was made, it could be argued that the marginalization of critical viewpoints in this case is less problematic than in the other Washington consensus cases.

On the other hand, the Gulf War is a clear case of strategic political calculations producing a consensus in support of U.S. policy that had not been the outcome of an assessment of its merits. One doubts that Democrats in Congress who emerged as supporters of the Gulf War on January 16 had suddenly decided that it constituted good policy. It is far more likely that the political imperatives of "supporting the troops" and of not being in the position of opposing a Republican war once it had started explain the change in the Democratic position. As experts outside of Washington had argued against going to war—and, not being politicians, had no reason to reverse their position when the war started—it is clear that critics were plentiful in the United States. It is true that a national debate had been conducted and the hawks had prevailed, but it is Democrats in Washington who made this debate a winner-take-all contest ending in the surrender of the defeated side; the media need not have reinforced this interpretation of its outcome.

Uncertain Intervention in Somalia

The marginalization of critical viewpoints on U.S. foreign policy in the news when there is consensus in Washington is a more interesting phenomenon than their appearance in the news when official actors are in conflict. Somalia and Haiti are of interest because they replicate the findings in the Grenada and the Gulf War (November) cases, which have

<hr/>

not, as I believe, a wise one." Anthony Lewis, "A Dark Trumpet," *New York Times,* January 25, 1991, A29.

[45] Anthony Lewis, "A Sense of Proportion," *New York Times,* January 28, 1991, A23.

been used to establish a benchmark for the analysis of the Washington consensus cases.

On *World News Tonight* and the *MacNeil/Lehrer Newshour*, Somalia looks about the same as the other Washington conflict cases. On the opinion pages of the *New York Times*, the figure for Somalia (67 percent) exceeds the other three by a substantial margin, but the total number of editorials and columns in the Somalia case—nine—is too small to interpret this finding as a meaningful one (although it is not hard to explain, as indicated below). Only in the news section of the *New York Times* does one find a significant departure from the general pattern. While the figures for Grenada, the Gulf War (November), and Haiti are clustered at 8.3 percent, 7.9 percent, and 7.1 percent, the figure for Somalia is much higher at 16.9 percent.[46] Based on over 1,300 paragraphs, this finding needs to be explained.

The Somalia case examined in the content analysis is the U.S. raid on the forces of Somali faction leader Mohammed Farah Aidid on October 3, 1993, an action that cost the U.S. significant casualties and sparked intense, focused opposition in the United States. This episode constituted the decisive turning point in the Somalia operation, forcing the Clinton administration to announce plans to withdraw U.S. troops within six months. Somalia is the one U.S. action examined in the content analysis that cannot be described (on its own terms) as a success. Although U.S. intervention in Grenada, the Persian Gulf (in November), and Haiti sparked opposition in Washington, in each case the White House executed the policy it had designed. In Somalia, however, U.S. policy failed.

The failure of U.S. foreign policy on its own terms, in itself, does not produce critical coverage if official actors do not speak out against it. Brody offers the Bay of Pigs invasion and the seizure of American hostages in Iran as examples of policy failures that (at first) generated neither criticism in Washington nor critical news coverage, and in fact *increased* public support for the president, until figures in Washington started to question U.S. policy.[47] In the Somalia case, however, Republicans and Democrats immediately denounced the U.S. raid on Aidid and demanded an end to the entire operation. The intensity of the opposition in Washington to Clinton's policy is described in *Congressional Quarterly:* "With a fury that neither administration officials nor their own leaders seemed able to control, lawmakers angrily clamored for Clinton to bring home all U.S. forces immedi-

---

[46] Coded as critical in this case were paragraphs criticizing the U.S. strategy of conducting a military offensive against hostile forces in Somalia; demanding that U.S. forces be withdrawn before Clinton planned to get them out; or otherwise expressing or indicating opposition to U.S. intervention in Somalia.

[47] Brody, *Assessing the President*, pp. 68–73.

ately."[48] In the aftermath of the unsuccessful raid, *CQ* reported "unease—bordering on contempt" toward Clinton's foreign policy in the Congress.[49]

One reason for this is that the U.S. action on October 3 appeared to contradict the strategy the administration had announced just days before. The *New York Times* explained:

> Faced in recent weeks with mounting Congressional opposition to the presence of American troops in Somalia, Administration officials said last week that the United States was moving away from the purely military goal of capturing and punishing General Aidid. Last month, Secretary of State Warren Christopher delivered a paper to Secretary General Boutros Boutros-Ghali of the United Nations detailing initiatives that would concentrate instead on political reconciliation.
>
> But in their public statements today, Administration officials were at a loss to explain why a military raid that left at least 12 American soldiers dead, dozens wounded and several others taken prisoner was conducted at the same time that Mr. Christopher was waging a campaign to persuade a reluctant Mr. Boutros-Ghali to pursue a political track aggressively.[50]

U.S. policy, in other words, appeared uncertain and confused, even on its own terms.

Adding to the confusion, the White House emitted contradictory signals on Somalia after the October 3 raid. On the one hand, Clinton ordered additional troops, tanks, and armored personnel carriers to Somalia and declared that the United States needed to show "firmness and steadiness of purpose."[51] On the other hand, U.S. policy changed, as "Mr. Clinton's advisers made clear that the United States no longer intended to make General Aidid the principal target,"[52] and the White House announced plans to end the entire operation on March 31, in effect abandoning the effort to achieve a military victory that had produced the debacle of October 3.

In contrast to Grenada, where Reagan offered a ringing justification of U.S. intervention; the November deployment to Saudi Arabia, where Bush declared the need for an offensive option against Iraq; and Haiti, where Clinton trumpeted a diplomatic victory, in Somalia the White House essentially abandoned its own policy, disavowing the very objective the Oc-

---

[48] Carroll J. Doherty, "Clinton Calms Rebellion on Hill by Retooling Somalia Mission," *Congressional Quarterly Weekly Report* 51, October 9, 1993, p. 2750.

[49] Pat Towell, "Behind Solid Vote on Somalia: A Hollow Victory for Clinton," *Congressional Quarterly Weekly Report* 51, October 16, 1993, p. 2823.

[50] Elaine Sciolino, "Puzzle in Somalia: The U.S. Goal," *New York Times*, October 5, 1993, A8.

[51] Thomas L. Friedman, "Clinton Sending More Troops to Somalia," *New York Times*, October 7, 1993, A1.

[52] Douglas Jehl, "Clinton Doubling U.S. Force in Somalia, Vowing Troops Will Come Home in 6 Months," *New York Times*, October 8, 1993, A1.

tober 3 raid had been designed to achieve. When the administration declined to mount much of a defense of its own policy, opponents of U.S. intervention seized the initiative, dealing the president a political defeat not seen in the other cases. This unique turn of events appears to explain the extraordinarily critical coverage in the Somalia case.

Clinton's speech outlining his new policy on October 7 won the support of major congressional figures such as Senators Dole and Nunn[53], and in the view of *Congressional Quarterly* "temporarily quelled a fractious rebellion in Congress."[54] Major pockets of opposition remained, however, as "key senators—including Democrat Bill Bradley of New Jersey and Republican John McCain of Arizona—rejected Clinton's retooled policy. [Democratic senator] Robert Byrd [of West Virginia] appeared determined to press ahead with an amendment . . . aimed at forcing a quick withdrawal from Somalia."[55] Byrd ended up supporting a Senate vote that affirmed the March 31 deadline Clinton had announced, but "even among senators who backed the successful amendment, there was derisive criticism of the Clinton team's handing of Somalia."[56]

This bipartisan congressional attack on a White House that had in effect disavowed its own policy produced a degree of critical coverage in the *New York Times* unmatched in the other three cases. On *World News Tonight*, the figure for Somalia exceeds those for the other Washington conflict cases, but just marginally. Why is the pattern in the *New York Times* not repeated on *World News Tonight*? In the case of Somalia, it turns out, ABC used almost exclusively official sources, failing to offer the usual story or two on the reaction of the mass public. A few such stories would have been enough to elevate the ABC figure to match the figure in the *Times*. During the same period, the *CBS Evening News* offered two stories on public reaction to U.S. intervention in Somalia. *NBC Nightly News* offered one such story and a studio report. Only ABC's *World News Tonight* failed to report public reaction to the Somalia debacle. The best explanation is that this is simply an anomaly.

The Odd Case of Haiti

The Clinton administration found itself in September 1994 on the brink of a second military action certain to generate opposition in Congress. Having tried for two years to get the military regime that had overthrown

[53] Ruth Marcus and Ann Devroy, "Clinton to Double Force in Somalia," *Washington Post*, October 8, 1993, A1.
[54] Doherty, "Clinton Calms Rebellion," p. 2750.
[55] Ibid.
[56] Towell, "Behind Solid Vote," p. 2823.

Haitian president Jean Bertrand Aristide in 1991 to step down, and needing to demonstrate the credibility of its threats, the White House moved toward military action in the summer of 1994. As it emerged that Clinton planned to use force to restore Aristide to power, Congress weighed in. *Congressional Quarterly* reported just before the intervention: "Congressional opposition to an invasion is extraordinarily broad. While conservative Republicans have been the most vocal critics, the opposition includes lawmakers from every point on the political spectrum."[57] In the context of this domestic political situation, Clinton struck a deal with the Haitian military leaders for a peaceful intervention.

This muted some of the opposition that had been expected in Congress. While Republicans continued to view the operation as misguided and believed that a Somalia-like scenario would unfold, "senior GOP lawmakers worried about overplaying their hand by excessively criticizing the president and the mission" at the outset.[58] "For all the criticism Congress has heaped on the military mission in Haiti," *Congressional Quarterly* wrote, "it appears reluctant to employ its legislative powers to interfere with President Clinton's policy in the troubled Caribbean nation."[59] Senate minority leader Robert Dole, for example, "was circulating [a] resolution that would declare that the United States has no national security interest in Haiti" but declined to back legislation mandating that the operation end on a specific date.[60]

Further complicating matters, while some who had been expected to oppose U.S. intervention declined to speak out or tempered their commentary, others who had been expected to support the operation turned out to be critics, as U.S. troops in Haiti watched as the very regime the White House had been set to overthrow continued to oppress the Haitian people.[61] This "triggered howls of protest on Capitol Hill,"[62] where some members opposed U.S. collaboration with the military regime. Although the White House quickly made adjustments to this policy, supporters of Aristide in the United States continued to point out the manifest contradictions in the operation. In sum, U.S. intervention in Haiti sparked sub-

[57] Carroll J. Doherty, "President, Rebuffing Congress, Prepares to Launch Invasion," *Congressional Quarterly Weekly Report* 52, September 17, 1994, p. 2582.

[58] Carroll J. Doherty, "As U.S. Troops Deploy Peacefully, Clinton's Battle Has Just Begun," *Congressional Quarterly Weekly Report* 52, September 24, 1994, p. 2705.

[59] Carroll J. Doherty, "Hill Wary of Putting Strings on Military Mission," *Congressional Quarterly Weekly Report* 52, October 1, 1994, p. 2816.

[60] Ibid., p. 2817.

[61] U.S. intervention in Saudi Arabia in August 1990 also caused some to argue for a more extensive military action (an offensive against Iraq), but those voices did support the initial military move. In the case of Haiti, liberal critics seemed to prefer no intervention at all to one conducted in collaboration with the military regime.

[62] Doherty, "U.S. Troops Deploy Peacefully," p. 2703.

THE RULE AND SOME EXCEPTIONS

stantial criticism from two directions in Congress, but not the clear and decisive opposition that had been expected.

Despite the unusual features of this case, it fits the pattern of the other Washington conflict cases (see table 5.1).[63] When U.S. intervention comes under fire in Washington, the *New York Times, World News Tonight*, and the *MacNeil/Lehrer Newshour* produce a substantial volume of critical coverage. Despite its idiosyncratic qualities, U.S. intervention in Haiti fits the pattern quite well.

The evidence in this book offers strong support for the indexing hypothesis. A few figures that do not match the general pattern have been investigated in this chapter. Opposition to the U.S. bombing of Libya inside the NATO alliance—made tangible in France's denial of its airspace to U.S. planes—appears to explain the unexpected number of critical *New York Times* columns and *MacNeil/Lehrer* guests in the Libya case. Coverage of antiwar demonstrations explains the higher percentage of critical paragraphs in the Gulf War (January) case, relative to the other Washington consensus cases, in the *New York Times* and on *World News Tonight*. The demonstrations were often reported, however, inside frames that undercut their message. U.S. intervention in Somalia produced the most critical coverage of the eight cases examined in the content analysis, because U.S. policy was a manifest failure and the president himself declined to speak with clear conviction in its defense.

[63] Paragraphs that criticized the restoration of Aristide to power; suggested that in negotiating the terms of U.S. intervention with the military regime, the U.S. had turned its back on the objective of restoring democracy in Haiti; or otherwise expressed or indicated opposition to U.S. intervention in Haiti were coded as critical.

Six

Television News and the Foreign-Policy Agenda

IT IS OFTEN argued that television news caused the United States to intervene in Somalia in 1992. Bernard C. Cohen writes that in the 1990s television

> has demonstrated its power to move governments. By focusing daily on the starving children in Somalia, a pictorial story tailor-made for television, TV mobilized the conscience of the nation's public institutions, compelling the government into a policy of intervention for humanitarian reasons.[1]

In the view of Michael Mandelbaum, "televised pictures of starving people" in Somalia "created a political clamor to feed them, which propelled the U.S. military" into action.[2] Adam Roberts characterizes U.S. intervention in Somalia as "Responding to the immediate pressure of media."[3] George F. Kennan describes American policy as "controlled by popular emotional impulses, and particularly ones provoked by the commercial television industry."[4]

Next to Vietnam, Somalia may be the most often cited case of media influence on American foreign policy. The argument that television contributed to the U.S. decision to intervene in Somalia is consistent with the chronology of events and news stories presented in this chapter. Somalia appeared on American television just before major changes in U.S. policy in August and November 1992, and these stories might well have influenced the decision of the Bush administration to act. What is not clear, however, is why Somalia appeared on television in the first place.

In the cases examined up to this point, it is easy to see why the events in question made the news. In the case of Somalia *before* the United States decided on military intervention, this is precisely what must be established. One possibility is that independent journalistic initiative put Soma-

[1] Bernard C. Cohen, "A View from the Academy," in Bennett and Paletz, *Taken by Storm*, pp. 9–10.

[2] Michael Mandelbaum, "The Reluctance to Intervene," *Foreign Policy* 95 (summer 1994): 16.

[3] Adam Roberts, "Humanitarian War: Military Intervention and Human Rights," *International Affairs* 69 (July 1993): 446.

[4] George F. Kennan, "Somalia, through a Glass Darkly," *New York Times*, September 30, 1993, A25.

lia on the news agenda. An example of this is television coverage of the Ethiopian famine in 1984. Immediately after a series of NBC stories on Ethiopia in October 1984, American aid to Ethiopia skyrocketed.[5] Harrison and Palmer show that an enterprising NBC correspondent in London is responsible for getting a story on Ethiopia originally broadcast on the BBC onto the air in the United States.[6] The origin of the Ethiopia story is found in the efforts of a journalist to publicize a distant event that had been essentially ignored in Washington and other Western capitals. The origin of Somalia as a news story could turn out to be similar.

A second possible explanation for the appearance of Somalia on American television is that it had not been ignored in Washington, but made the news only after it had generated substantial interest there. In this scenario, television coverage of Somalia in the summer and fall of 1992 originated not in the independent initiative of journalists, but in the interaction of journalists engaged in routine newsgathering practices and sources in Washington who made efforts to get Somalia onto the news agenda. If the evidence matches this description, then U.S. intervention in Somalia is not a case of the media setting the foreign-policy agenda, but instead is further evidence of the impact of official actors on the news.

Although the Ethiopia model is implicit in claims that television news got America into Somalia, the evidence indicates that not until Washington had turned its attention to Somalia did ABC, CBS, and NBC deem events there worthy of coverage. If television contributed to the U.S. decision to act, it did so under the influence of governmental actors—a number of senators, a House committee, a presidential candidate, and figures within the Bush administration—who made efforts to publicize events in Somalia, interpret them as constituting a crisis, and encourage a U.S. response. The lesson of Somalia is not just about the influence of television on Washington; it is also about the influence of Washington on television.

Background and Overview

At the beginning of 1992, civil war and starvation gripped Somalia, in the wake of the overthrow of Mohammed Siad Barre, who had ruled the country for two decades. In January, the United Nations Security Council passed a resolution calling for a cease-fire and a political settlement of the

[5] Christopher J. Bosso, "Setting the Agenda: Mass Media and the Discovery of Famine in Ethiopia," in Margolis and Mauser, *Manipulating Public Opinion*, pp. 168–69.

[6] Paul Harrison and Robin Palmer, *News Out of Africa: Biafra to Band Aid* (London: Hilary Shipman, 1986), pp. 123–24.

conflict.[7] In March this cease-fire went into effect; but with no national government and continued factional conflict over food, by August "as many as 1.5 million of an estimated Somali population of 6 million were threatened with starvation, with approximately 300,000 Somalis already having died, including roughly 25 percent of all children under the age of five."[8]

As of March, the United States resisted a peacekeeping role for the United Nations in Somalia, supporting a Security Council resolution "only after language calling for a UN-sponsored peace-keeping mission had been removed."[9] In April, the Security Council authorized a modest military operation, but negotiations with Somali factions delayed its implementation. On July 27, the Security Council voted to airlift food to Somalia, and on August 12 the U.N. announced plans to send 500 troops to protect the international relief effort. On August 14, the White House announced that the United States would take charge of the airlift.[10]

The 500 troops arrived in September—"with the support of four U.S. warships carrying 2,100 Marines"—but proved unable to do much to protect the relief effort.[11] In November, U.N. secretary general Boutros Boutros-Ghali notified the Security Council that the relief effort was not working. On November 26, the Bush administration announced that the United States would send troops to Somalia if the Security Council passed an authorizing resolution, which it did on December 3. The first contingent of Operation Restore Hope hit the shores of Somalia on December 9.

The focus here is on coverage of Somalia on ABC's *World News Tonight*, *CBS Evening News*, *NBC Nightly News*, and CNN from January 1 through November 25 of 1992, the day before the White House announced plans for U.S. intervention. I focus on television because it is the emotional impact of television pictures, not the information reported in newspaper stories, that is said to have inspired American intervention in Somalia. I look first at the three major networks, then at CNN, for two reasons. First, ABC, CBS, and NBC each have an audience over 10 times the size of CNN's and are therefore more likely to influence official estimates of public opinion. Second, the coverage on CNN differs from what is found on the major networks in one quite interesting way.

---

[7] Samuel M. Makinda, *Seeking Peace from Chaos: Humanitarian Intervention in Somalia* (Boulder, Colo.: Lynne Rienner, 1993), p. 61.

[8] Peter J. Schraeder, *United States Foreign Policy toward Africa: Incrementalism, Crisis, and Change* (Cambridge: Cambridge University Press, 1994), p. 177.

[9] Ibid., p. 170.

[10] Makinda, *Seeking Peace from Chaos*, pp. 62–63; Schraeder, *Foreign Policy toward Africa*, p. 175.

[11] Schraeder, *Foreign Policy toward Africa*, p. 175.

TABLE 6.1

Coverage of Somalia on ABC, CBS, and NBC in 1992

	Time in Minutes	Stories over 30 Seconds
January	1.5	1
February	2.0	1
March	2.5	1
April	0.0	0
May	0.3	0
June	0.2	0
July	5.7	2
August	48.3	18
September	13.0	6
October	3.8	1
November	16.3	4

Source: Television News Index and Abstracts.

Note: For entries with multiple subjects (not just Somalia), time listed is divided by the number of subjects. November figures are for November 1–25.

TABLE 6.2

Five Phases of Somalia Coverage on ABC, CBS, and NBC in 1992

Phase	Dates	Total Time (minutes)	Time per Week (minutes)
1	January 1–July 21	6.5	0.2
2	July 22–August 13	15.4	4.7
3	August 14–September 18	55.3	10.8
4	September 19–November 8	4.2	0.6
5	November 9–November 25	16.3	6.7

Source: Television News Index and Abstracts.

If the evening news influenced the U.S. decision to intervene, when could this influence have been exerted? Table 6.1 displays the time and the number of stories on Somalia on ABC, CBS, and NBC from January to November 1992.

The table shows an extraordinarily low level of coverage from January through June, averaging about one minute per month on the three networks combined; an increase in July; extensive coverage in August and September; a sharp drop-off in October; and a rebound in November. The distribution of coverage is more clearly illustrated when it is divided into five phases, corresponding to clusters in the data. This is done in table 6.2.

In phase 1—January 1 to July 21—Somalia is close to invisible on the major networks, averaging just 12 seconds of coverage per week. In phase 2—July 22 to August 13—the coverage increased to over 4 minutes per week. In phase 3—August 14 to September 18—Somalia received extensive coverage, over 10 minutes per week, focusing on the American airlift. In phase 4—September 19 to November 8—Somalia disappeared from view, the coverage falling to under a minute per week. In phase 5— November 9 to November 25—Somalia returned from the eclipse of phase 4 (although not returning to the level of phase 3), to about 7 minutes per week.

Phase 2 ends with the announcement of the U.S. airlift to Somalia on August 14. Phase 5 ends with the announcement of military intervention on November 26. As phases 1 and 4 contain almost no coverage of Somalia, it is in phases 2 and 5 that the search for television's influence on U.S. intervention must be conducted.

The August Airlift Decision

From January 1 to July 21, six stories on Somalia appeared on the three major networks. Three were studio reports that averaged under 20 seconds in length. The other three, full stories of 70 to 150 seconds, appeared on January 5, February 27, and March 2 (a full story is one reported by a correspondent, as opposed to a studio report read by the anchor).[12] CBS reported on February 27 that "half of Somalia's eight million people may die of starvation,"[13] and NBC on March 2 described "a terrible, closed world of violence and destruction."[14] As this series of stories ends five months before August, however, it is unlikely that it made a significant contribution to the events of the summer (although the possibility of some minor influence on the evolution of American policy is not ruled out).

Not until July is the next full story on Somalia broadcast on the major networks. From July 22 to August 13, there are nine stories on Somalia. Five of the nine, studio reports that do not exceed 20 seconds in length, are not serious candidates for influence on American policy. The four full stories, however, require further investigation. All contained video of starving Somalis. Table 6.3 superimposes events in Washington in the

[12] The full stories in this chapter average two to three minutes in length. No studio report exceeds 30 seconds.

[13] *CBS Evening News*, February 27, 1992.

[14] *NBC Nightly News*, March 2, 1992.

TABLE 6.3
Chronology of Events and Stories Relating to Intervention in Somalia,
July and August 1992

July 19	Senator Simon calls for action
July 22	Senator Kassebaum calls for action
July 22	House Select Committee on Hunger conducts hearings
July 22	*ABC Story*
July 23	Senator Kennedy suggests action
July 27	White House calls for "urgent attention"
July 31	*CBS Story*
August 3	Senate resolution
August 6	Senator McConnell compares Somalia to Bosnia
August 7	Senator Jeffords compares Somalia to Bosnia
August 8	President Bush mentions Somalia at news conference
August 9	Senator Rockefeller criticizes Bush
August 10	House Resolution
August 12	U.N. announces plan to send troops
August 13	Bill Clinton mentions Somalia as foreign-policy issue
August 13	*ABC Stories*
August 14	White House announces airlift

month before the decision to conduct an airlift over the timing of the four full stories on Somalia.

The first full story in this period—and the first since March 2—appeared on ABC on July 22. It described and showed pictures of the grim situation in Somalia, a country of "six million people waiting for relief, starving for attention."[15] Before credit for putting Somalia on the foreign-policy agenda is allocated to television, however, it is necessary to examine the context of official activities in which the story appeared. On July 22, the day the story aired, the House Select Committee on Hunger had held hearings on Somalia, at which Senator Nancy Kassebaum, who had been chair of the Subcommittee on Africa of the Senate Foreign Relations Committee when the Republicans controlled the Senate from 1981 to 1986, and just returned from an official visit to Somalia, testified that the situation there was desperate and declared, "I strongly support sending a

[15] *World News Tonight*, July 22, 1992.

United Nations security force to Somalia."[16] This declaration, reported in
the ABC story, clashed with the position of the Bush administration that
a U.N. force should not be deployed until a cease-fire had been achieved
among the Somali factions. On the Democratic side, Senator Paul Simon,
chair of the Subcommittee on Africa since 1987, had commended Kassebaum for going to Somalia and urged the White House to act: "I don't
want to wait to have a Democratic administration before we respond more
adequately. I want to do it now."[17]

The events of July 22 do not represent the first notice of Somalia in
Washington in 1992, but they do mark the movement of the story into a
new phase, one of direct calls for forceful action.[18] Although Congress had
expressed concern about Somalia in the spring, it had not challenged the
Bush administration's policy of working through the U.N. to achieve a
diplomatic solution. A resolution introduced in the House in April commended the administration "for its significant efforts to provide food and
humanitarian relief to Somalia."[19] A resolution in the Senate in May expressed "the sense of the Senate regarding needed action to address the
continuing state of war and chaos and the emergency humanitarian situation in Somalia," but suggested no change in policy.[20] In other words,
Congress in the spring simply instructed the White House and the U.N.
to go forward with existing policy, hardly a newsworthy event in the
framework of American journalism, which most often finds news where
there is conflict, or something that moves a story forward.[21] Conflict and
movement were not present until July, when Kassebaum and Simon declared the response of the Bush administration inadequate and urged a
change in policy.

ABC's July 22 story is best understood as a joint production of politicians, who made efforts to publicize the crisis in Somalia and the possibility
of some form of U.S. intervention, and journalists, who decided to respond to those efforts with coverage.[22] The decision at ABC to broadcast
the story may have been influenced by the judgment that the visually stun-
ning Somalia story made "good television" and could hold an audience,

[16] Ibid.
[17] Marilyn Greene, "Senator Reaches Out to Somalia," *USA Today,* July 20, 1992, 6A.
[18] On the use of "phase structures" to determine what constitutes news, see Fishman,
Manufacturing the News, pp. 63–76.
[19] *Congressional Record,* April 7, 1992, E978.
[20] *Congressional Record,* May 19, 1992, S6933.
[21] Fishman, *Manufacturing the News,* pp. 63–76.
[22] On the news as a joint production of sources and journalists, see Timothy E. Cook,
Making Laws and Making News: Media Strategies in the U.S. House of Representatives (Washington, D.C.: Brookings Institution, 1989).

or the conviction that television—which had inspired efforts to aid Ethiopia eight years earlier—had a responsibility to publicize massive human suffering. It is economic factors that are invoked when reference is made to "the commercial television industry"[23] as the source of U.S. interest in Somalia; ideological factors are suggested in the assertion that journalists "mobilized the conscience of the nation's public institutions,"[24] presumably acting out of conscience themselves.

Economic and ideological factors might well have contributed to ABC's decision to send cameras to Somalia. But the timing of the story points to the influence of Senators Kassebaum and Simon, and the House Committee on Hunger, in getting Somalia considered as a possible story in the first place.[25] Contrary to the impression created by those who attribute to television "the power to move governments,"[26] ABC seems to have observed a rule of deference to government officials, in this case the top Senate experts on Africa in terms of institutional position, in deciding that events in Somalia constituted news in the United States. The efforts of Kassebaum and Simon to publicize the crisis in Somalia were not *sufficient* to get the story on television—ABC had to cooperate, a decision economic, ideological, and other factors could have contributed to—but the evidence clearly suggests that those efforts were *necessary*. As I show below, precisely the same pattern is found in November, Somalia turning up on television after a period of near invisibility on the very day that a congressional delegation reported on a visit to Somalia and urged U.S. action.

As of July 22, Somalia had not attained a very conspicuous position on the foreign-policy agenda; two senators and a House committee constitute just one corner of the Washington foreign-policy establishment. If ABC had made Somalia the top story, or had offered a series of stories on it in July, a case could be made that it had been magnified out of proportion to its place on the Washington agenda. As Harrison and Palmer observe of British coverage of Ethiopia in 1984, "by leading on two consecutive days with items of eight and seven minutes in length . . . the BBC was quite clearly saying: 'Here is an event of major importance.' "[27] Yet the

[23] Kennan, "Through a Glass Darkly." On news as entertainment, see Neil Postman, *Amusing Ourselves to Death: Public Discourse in the Age of Show Business* (New York: Penguin Books, 1985).

[24] Cohen, "View from the Academy," p. 10.

[25] Relief agencies inside the U.S. government had also made efforts to get journalists to report the disaster in Somalia before it appeared on television. On the role of the U.S. government's relief agencies, see Steven Livingston and Todd Eachus, "Humanitarian Crises and U.S. Foreign Policy: Somalia and the CNN Effect Reconsidered," *Political Communication* 12 (October–December 1995): 413–29.

[26] Cohen, "View from the Academy," p. 9.

[27] Harrison and Palmer, *News Out of Africa*, p. 129.

ABC story appeared in isolation, at the end of *World News Tonight*. Somalia may not have been at the top of the foreign-policy agenda in July, but neither did it appear at the top of the news.

"Somalia," CBS reported on July 31, "is in danger of becoming a vast graveyard."[28] In Washington, this turn of events had not gone unnoticed. On July 27, the *Washington Post* reported: "Congressional pressure is mounting to send U.N. peacekeeping troops to guard relief shipments to Somalia."[29] Senator Edward Kennedy, for example, wondered "why we're not moving in Somalia as we are in Yugoslavia."[30] White House spokesman Marlin Fitzwater indicated on July 27 that Somalia was on the president's agenda: "The tragedy in Somalia . . . requires the urgent attention of the international community."[31] In other words, CBS covered Somalia on July 31—the first story on CBS since February 27—after officials in Washington had defined it as a significant concern of American foreign policy. Instead of being out ahead of Washington, television appears to have acted in concert with Congress and the White House in illuminating events in Somalia.

This is the only story on Somalia over 20 seconds in length on the major networks in the 21 days from July 23 to August 12. If television contributed to the evolution of American interest in Somalia in this period, its contribution must be described (at best) as measured and proportionate. Far from magnifying the crisis, ABC, CBS, and NBC responded to the White House declaration on July 27 that Somalia warranted "urgent attention" with one story on one network on July 31, near the end of the broadcast, and no further stories until August 13.

As one moves into August, it appears that Washington is getting out ahead of television on Somalia. On August 3, the Senate passed a resolution urging the deployment of a U.N. force to Somalia. A similar resolution passed the House on August 10.[32] From August 3 to August 13, four more senators and a presidential candidate addressed Somalia. Senator Jay Rockefeller listed Somalia as one of four examples of the failure of Bush's foreign policy and criticized the president for inaction: "What's he doing about Somalia? . . . [T]here's no planning. There's no sense of a course."[33]

[28] *CBS Evening News*, July 31, 1992.

[29] Shari Rudavsky, "Bush, U.N. Face Pressure to Aid War-Torn Somalia," *Washington Post*, July 27, 1992, A18.

[30] "Hearing of the Senate Judiciary Committee: U.S. Refugee Programs for FY 1993," *Federal News Service*, July 23, 1992.

[31] "Statement by Press Secretary Fitzwater on the Situation in Somalia," *Public Papers of the Presidents*, July 27, 1992.

[32] Schraeder, *Foreign Policy toward Africa*, p. 177. Unlike the spring resolutions, which had not criticized existing policy, the August resolutions called for a change in policy.

[33] *Newsmaker Sunday*, CNN, August 9, 1992.

Somalia also appeared in the debate over Bosnia, which heated up in early August. On August 5, six senators demanded U.S. action on Bosnia, and on August 13 the Security Council passed a resolution authorizing the use of force to deliver aid to Sarajevo and other areas. Somalia was introduced into this debate by opponents of intervention in Bosnia. Senator James Jeffords wondered: "How do you make distinctions between going into the former Yugoslavia, . . . and Somalia?"[34] Senator Mitch McConnell also argued that intervention in Bosnia could be a slippery slope leading to intervention in Somalia.[35] In responding to this argument, supporters of intervention in Bosnia, like Senator Joseph Lieberman, noted the gravity of the crisis in Somalia and indicated that further action might be required there too.[36] In other words, the juxtaposition of Bosnia and Somalia in U.S. foreign-policy debate emerged in part from the tactics of opponents of intervention in Bosnia in the Senate. Finally, on August 13, Democratic presidential candidate Bill Clinton cited Somalia—along with Bosnia and Cambodia—as a "torn" area in which "multilateral action holds promise as never before."[37]

Only after all this do the first stories on Somalia in August appear, on ABC on August 13. One story described Somalia as "on the verge of committing suicide," a country in a state of "utter and complete and hopeless misery," where one finds "Graves in athletic fields. Graves in farm fields. Graves along city streets." A second story in the same broadcast explored why the West appeared more interested in Bosnia than Somalia. An official from Transafrica argued: "it's as if the U.S. government is saying that the lives of black babies are not as important and that suffering Bosnians are worth more . . . than the starving Somalians."[38]

On August 14, the White House announced plans to airlift emergency aid to Somalia. It is at this point that the case for the influence of television appears strongest.[39] On August 12, the United Nations had announced that the warring Somali factions had consented to the deployment of 500 U.N. troops to guard relief supplies, indicating an increase in the international effort to aid Somalia. This could have encouraged ABC to frame a story around the emerging international *response* to the crisis. Instead, ABC focused on why the West had *not* responded.

---

[34] *Morning Edition*, NPR, August 7, 1992.

[35] *MacNeil/Lehrer Newshour*, August 6, 1992.

[36] *Crossfire*, CNN, August 3, 1992.

[37] "Excerpts from Clinton's Speech on Foreign Policy Leadership," *New York Times*, August 14, 1992, A15.

[38] *World News Tonight*, August 13, 1992.

[39] Although Livingston and Eachus report that the Bush administration decided on the airlift on August 12, the day *before* the August 13 stories on ABC. Livingston and Eachus, "Humanitarian Crises," p. 426.

ABC's decision must be understood in the context of the international response to the crisis in Bosnia. The Security Council had just passed a resolution authorizing the *use of force* to deliver humanitarian aid in Bosnia. Although there were questions about the likelihood of its implementation, reports indicated that NATO had been engaged in "operational planning" and that over 100,000 troops could participate.[40] Next to this effort to show international resolve on Bosnia, a plan to send just 500 troops to Somalia to guard relief supplies, not even authorized to use force to deliver them to those in need, must have seemed unimpressive. The international effort on Somalia paled at this point next to the far greater effort that appeared to be in the works on Bosnia, a contrast American politicians, as noted, had been working to illuminate. Somalia had figured in Washington debate as the crisis the world had ignored, and the announcement of a major international initiative on Bosnia just 24 hours after reports of a minor one on Somalia simply reinforced this interpretation.

It is not hard to explain why the United States finally acted on Somalia. In addition to principled concern for the Somali people and the "new world order" the president may have had, an administration official cited "a desire by the White House to initiate a dramatic relief effort on the eve of the Republican national convention."[41] According to this official, "The White House figured they couldn't gain votes by acting in Somalia but their image could be tarnished if they didn't do anything." Of course, political costs from inaction only come into play if the inaction is publicized, and in framing events in Somalia in a way that supported the case for intervention, ABC may have influenced the decision the White House made. Yet if ABC influenced U.S. policy in crystallizing and amplifying the political stakes in Somalia, it is American politics (and events in Bosnia) that created those stakes in the first place, as well as the frame through which ABC interpreted events in Somalia and the U.S. response.

In sum, an assessment of the scope and character of television's influence on U.S. foreign policy in the summer of 1992 must weigh the evidence that as of August 13, ABC had received numerous signals from actors in Washington—seven senators, a House committee, the full House and Senate, the Democratic candidate for president, and the White House— that Somalia had emerged as a subject of foreign-policy debate in Washington. This debate, like the ABC stories on August 13, focused on the proposition that U.S. policy toward Somalia stood in contrast to U.S.

---

[40] Trevor Rowe, "U.N. Approves Use of Military Force for Bosnia Aid," *Washington Post,* August 14, 1992, A1.

[41] Jane Perlez, "U.S. Encounters Snags in Airlift to Aid Somalia," *New York Times,* August 22, 1992, p. 1.

policy toward Bosnia, an assessment the Bush administration made no great effort to dispute. ABC could have found another way to frame its Somalia coverage, but only if it had rejected the frame that had emerged in Washington.

As the August 13 stories on Somalia are the first to exceed 20 seconds in length on ABC, CBS, or NBC in August, it is hard to argue that television magnified Somalia out of proportion to the interest it had generated in Washington. As in July, the volume of coverage is consistent with (if not less than) what journalistic routines geared to official sources could have been expected to produce.

When Kennan describes U.S. policy as "controlled by popular emotional impulses, . . . provoked by the commercial television industry,"[42] the implication is that television framed Somalia in a way that inspired an emotional reaction. Indeed, the coverage does at times seem to have been designed to pull at the heartstrings and create a sense of American responsibility, as in ABC's August 13 presentation of "a bewildered little girl," her family dead, "waiting like so many others for help that may never come" from a world that has "turned its back on this country."[43] This is an angle the Bush administration, gearing up for the fall campaign, must have found disturbing.

Although explicit commentary on the failure of the West to act is not necessary for a story to push U.S. policy in that direction—pictures of dying children can speak for themselves—it is noteworthy that the framing of the crisis in Somalia as a humanitarian disaster *the United States could do something about* does not appear on television until it had appeared in Washington first. Stories in February and March, before senators had criticized the White House for not acting, characterized Somalia as "a terrible, *closed* world of violence and destruction,"[44] the language offering no hint of possible U.S. intervention. This is a frame that evokes, in contrast to the one found in July, a sense of inevitability and hopelessness about the events described.

In July, when Kassebaum called on the United States and the international community to do more for Somalia and criticized White House inaction, this angle started to appear on television. The framing of Somalia as desperate for Western intervention that *could happen* turns out to be a joint production of television journalists and actors in Washington, who signaled in July and August that the crisis in Somalia was not just an unfortunate disaster in a distant land, but one the United States could do something about.

---

[42] Kennan, "Through a Glass Darkly."

[43] *World News Tonight*, August 13, 1992.

[44] *NBC Nightly News*, March 2, 1992, emphasis added.

A CNN Effect?

For the most part, the coverage on CNN followed the pattern found on ABC, CBS, and NBC. From June 1 to August 13, only three stories on Somalia appeared on CNN: on July 27, August 4, and August 6, or after Somalia had emerged as a contested issue in Washington. From January 1 to April 30, CNN offered no stories on Somalia. Where CNN departs from the pattern observed on the major networks is in May. Without any apparent cues from Washington, CNN sent a reporter to Somalia and presented eight stories on the crisis there from May 1 to May 15.

In this series of reports we find the stuff of which the image of television's power over U.S. foreign policy is made. Pictures of starving Somalis illustrate the following narrative:

> The weak were pushed aside, trampled in the rush on one rice pot. The cooks desperately tried to save it as the starving crowd clawed in vain. Hundreds of faces eyed the cooking pot, burning to eat the contents.[45]

> These are the faces of famine. Countless thousands of children now look like this. Hanging on to life by a thread, hoping that something soon will change. They want the world to see, to witness their skeletal forms, to share and understand their agony, and to forcefully act in a way that will end or at least ease this suffering.[46]

The detail here is more vivid, more disturbing, than in the CBS and NBC stories in February and March. Moreover, in contrast to the CBS and NBC stories, CNN explicitly framed Somalia as a tragedy the United States had turned its back on, ignoring those children who "want the world to see . . . and to forcefully act." In the blunt assessment of CNN's Brent Sadler, Somalia "needs bombarding with food by a massive, coordinated rescue mission,"[47] and [the West] "will be neither forgiven nor forgotten"[48] if this does not happen. Finally, eight reports in two weeks made Somalia a major story on CNN, two months before the Kassebaum visit, and three months before the U.S. airlift.

In the first half of May, CNN presented the crisis in Somalia in extraordinarily dire terms and explicitly criticized Western nations for declining to act. Yet the CNN stories had no discernable impact on American policy. Plans to increase the U.N. presence in Somalia continued to stall. The call for intervention was not echoed in Washington. Nor were demands for

[45] "Somalians Fight over Meager Rations," CNN, May 11, 1992.
[46] "Somalian Famine Reaches Crisis Proportions," CNN, May 15, 1992.
[47] "Somalia Starvation Worsens Due to Civil War," CNN, May 3, 1992.
[48] "Somalia Problems Mounting without Signs of Respite," CNN, May 5, 1992.

U.S. action being made around the United States, if letters to the editor are an indication: a LEXIS/NEXIS search of letters to nine major American newspapers turned up one letter on Somalia in May, one in June, and one in July.[49] Not until August did the number of letters to the editor in the nine newspapers increase (to 25). Although editors have the power to decide what subjects to publish letters on, if the CNN stories in May had generated a significant public outcry, one might have expected the letters in *some* of the papers examined to reflect this.

In sum, the series of stories on CNN in May offers a test: What happens when television *does* independently investigate a foreign crisis that has not sparked much interest in Washington and frames it in terms that cry out for action? In this case, there is no evidence of an impact on U.S. policy.

It is possible that the CNN stories had some behind-the-scenes influence on Senator Kassebaum and others in Washington, perhaps encouraging them to believe that interest in Somalia could be mobilized in the United States down the road. Yet what influence CNN might have had in the spring is far more subtle and indirect than declarations on "the immediate pressure of media"[50] and claims that television "propelled the U.S. military"[51] into action would suggest. Although CNN could perhaps have made some small contribution to the evolution of Washington's interest in Somalia, the stories in May are evidence that even a concerted effort on the part of CNN to put a foreign crisis on the Washington agenda can be without discernable impact on U.S. policy if the "pressure of media" is not joined with a political dynamic that encourages action. Of course, if ABC, CBS, or NBC, each with an audience over 10 times the size of CNN's, had broadcast eight stories on Somalia in May, the impact on the public—and on politicians who anticipate the evolution of public opinion—could have been much greater.

The November Ground Troop Decision

Somalia received substantial television coverage for about a month after August 13. From August 14 to September 18, the three major networks devoted over 55 minutes to Somalia, or about 18 minutes per network. The stories reported preparations for the airlift of food to Somalia, the

---

[49] The papers were selected arbitrarily: they are the nine papers that list their letters in LEXIS/NEXIS under the heading "letters to the editor." The papers are the *Columbus Dispatch, Louisville Courier-Journal, San Diego Union-Tribune, San Francisco Chronicle, Atlanta Journal and Constitution, Los Angeles Times, Orlando Sentinel Tribune, St. Petersburg Times,* and *Washington Post.* The search terms were *letters to the editor* and *Somalia.*

[50] Roberts, "Humanitarian War," pp. 446.

[51] Mandelbaum, "The Reluctance to Intervene," p. 16.

TABLE 6.4
Chronology of Events and Stories Relating to Intervention in Somalia,
November 1992

November 9	Senators Simon, Kassebaum, and Wofford call for further action
November 18	Bush-Clinton meeting addresses Somalia; Bush aides consider further action; congressional delegation holds press conference in Nairobi
November 18	*ABC Story*
November 21	Congressional delegation holds press conference in Washington
November 21	*CBS Story, NBC Story*
November 24	*NBC Story*
November 26	White House announces plan to send troops

operation itself, and the pitfalls it encountered. Most of the stories contained video from Somalia. As the United States was conducting a military operation there, it is hard to argue that this coverage magnified Somalia out of proportion to its place on the foreign-policy agenda. Moreover, despite U.S. military activity in Somalia and an ample supply of video footage of starving children, not once was Somalia the top story on ABC, CBS, or NBC in the January 1 to November 25 period.

On September 18, the United States temporarily suspended flights to one area of Somalia after an aircraft came under fire. Although the airlift continued, at this point Somalia all but vanished from the news. From September 19 to November 8, just 250 seconds of coverage appeared on the major networks. The primary reason for the eclipse of Somalia on American television is the presidential election in the United States, in which foreign policy played a marginal role. With a campaign focused on domestic issues, politicians for the most part ignored Somalia, offering journalists few words or deeds upon which stories might have been based. In addition, the story simply grew old, as the airlift went on with no change of phase to generate "news" deemed worthy of coverage.[52]

From November 9 to November 25 (the day before the White House announced plans to send troops), over 16 minutes of Somalia coverage appeared on ABC, CBS, and NBC. From November 9 to November 17, this took the form of six studio reports (or brief mentions in stories on other subjects) of 10 to 30 seconds in length. The coverage then increased, as four full stories appeared from November 18 to November 24. Table 6.4 displays the four full stories in November, juxtaposed with activities in Congress and at the White House.

[52] Fishman, *Manufacturing the News*, pp. 63–76.

The first reference to Somalia in November, a brief mention in an ABC story on President-elect Clinton's military policy, appeared the day Senators Simon, Kassebaum, and Harris Wofford held a press conference urging further U.S. action on Somalia. "The United Nations has to move from being peacekeeper to being a peacemaker," Simon declared. "This is a situation that cannot wait" for Clinton to take office. Senator Kassebaum argued: "We simply must send security guards in."[53] In mentioning Somalia on November 9, ABC clearly had not gotten out ahead of Washington.

On November 18, Clinton met with President Bush at the White House for a briefing that focused on foreign affairs. After the meeting Clinton cited four areas of the world that had been discussed: the former Soviet republics, Bosnia, the North American Free Trade Area, and Somalia.[54] The Clinton camp was struck by the depth of Bush's concern over Somalia.[55] The *New York Times* reported in a story written the same day, "Key Bush aides will . . . urge [the president] to energize the U.N. now to provide more food, more transport and most importantly more troops with more powerful weapons and a mandate to be aggressive."[56] Also on November 18, a six-member congressional delegation that had just visited Somalia held a press conference in Nairobi, describing the situation in Somalia as "an affront to humanity" that demanded further action.[57]

Not until the White House had put Somalia at the top of its agenda and Congress had dispatched a delegation to investigate the crisis did the first full story on Somalia appear in November, on ABC on November 18. Neither White House nor congressional activities are reported in the story, which focuses on the futility of U.N. efforts in Somalia to this point, but as in July, the timing points to a connection. In November as in July, the evening news first broadcast a story on Somalia the very day a congressional delegation reported on a visit to that country and called for U.S. intervention. In each case, television coverage and the actions of politicians are closely correlated, official actions falling immediately before Somalia makes the news.

Three more stories appeared on the major networks before the announcement of the decision to send U.S. troops. Half of the November 21 story on NBC is an interview with Representative John Lewis, head of the congressional delegation to Somalia, who argues: "We must get the

[53] Marilyn Greene, "Senators Call for Protection for Somalian Aid Shipments," *USA Today*, November 10, 1992, 6A.

[54] Gwen Ifill, "Bush and Clinton Proclaim End to the Election's Rancor," *New York Times*, November 19, 1992, A22.

[55] Russell Watson, "Troops to Somalia," *Newsweek*, December 7, 1992, p. 24.

[56] Leslie H. Gelb, "Shoot to Feed Somalia," *New York Times*, November 19, 1992, A27.

[57] Buchizya Mseteka, "Members of Congress Call for Firmer U.N. Role in Somalia," Reuters, November 18, 1992.

United States to go before the U.N. and intervene."[58] The CBS story on
November 21 also focuses on the findings of the congressional delegation.[59] The November 21 stories may have accelerated the movement in
Washington toward intervention, but they are also clearly a product of
that movement.

Only after all of this does what was probably the most powerful and
evocative story about Somalia on the major networks appear. On November 24, NBC presented a series of still photographs of starvation in Somalia, over the grim narration of anchor Tom Brokaw:

> In Somalia, children under the age of five have all but disappeared. Hundreds
> die each week. It's a place where a thousand die today, and a thousand will die
> tomorrow, and the day after that, and the day after that. We have seen all this
> before, and we will see it again. The images will fade, but the memory cannot.[60]

It is reasonable to suppose that pictures and commentary of this nature
on the evening news would have increased the sense of the White House
that something had to be done about Somalia, or the legacy of the Bush
administration and its "new world order" could be tarnished.[61] In assessing television's influence, however, it is important to note that the tone
of this report is no more dire than the judgment of Representative Lewis,
whom the House had sent to Somalia, that what he had found there
"[could not] be compared to anything else in modern history."[62] NBC's
grim framing of Somalia, it turns out, matches that of the institutionally
authorized representative of the House.

CNN's coverage in November parallels the major networks. The first
CNN story in November appeared on the 12th. The Somali fashion model
Iman is interviewed and urges further action. Yet it does not appear that
CNN made an entirely independent decision to consult Iman, as just three
days earlier Senators Kassebaum and Simon had held a press conference
with her, marking Iman—not otherwise likely to have been viewed as a
credible source of opinion on U.S. foreign policy—as worthy of consulta-
tion. Stories on Somalia also appeared on CNN on November 15, 22, and
24, in a pattern similar to the one found on the major networks.

In view of the position Somalia had achieved on the American foreign-
policy agenda, it is hard to argue that television overplayed the story in
November. ABC and CBS each found space from November 1 to November 25 for a single story on Somalia exceeding 30 seconds in length, nei-

[58] *NBC Nightly News,* November 21, 1992.
[59] *CBS Evening News,* November 21, 1992.
[60] *NBC Nightly News,* November 24, 1992.
[61] On this danger, see Jim Mann, "Somalia Closing Out Bush's 'New World Order,'" *Los Angeles Times,* November 29, 1992, A1.
[62] "Rep. John Lewis," *Reuter Transcript Report,* November 21, 1992.

ther in the top half of the broadcast. NBC offered two full stories on Somalia, neither in the top third of the news. Setting aside brief studio reports and mentions of Somalia in other stories that could not possibly be argued to have influenced the decision of the Bush administration to act, one is left with four stories on Somalia on ABC, CBS, and NBC over 25 days. This is hardly a record of overplaying what the head of a congressional delegation had described as without precedent in modern history, and what President-elect Clinton, following a meeting with President Bush, had identified as one of four major issues on the foreign-policy agenda of the United States.

Events in Somalia could not have threatened to inflict political damage on George Bush in August, or to tarnish his legacy in November, had they not been publicized in the United States. The August 13 stories on ABC may have signaled to the White House the political dangers that lurked if it failed to act on an issue that Democrats (and some Republicans) had begun to use against it,[63] and news stories in November may have crystallized the damage the president's place in history could suffer if the "new world order" proved to be meaningless for Somalia. But if television contributed to the emergence of Somalia as a political liability for the president in August and a threat to his legacy in November, it had powerful, outspoken allies in Washington whose efforts to get Somalia onto the news in the first place were essential. Stories on Somalia were broadcast just after the articulation of demands for U.S. intervention in Washington in the summer and fall of 1992. Journalists made the final decision to cover Somalia, of course, but the stage for this decision had been set in Washington. The case of U.S. intervention in Somalia, in sum, is not at heart evidence of the power of television to move governments; it is evidence of the power of governments to move television.

The Origins of Television's Interest in Bosnia

A second case that has been offered as evidence of the impact of television news on the American foreign-policy agenda is the war in Bosnia upon the division of Yugoslavia. As of May 1992, Bosnia had emerged as a major story on American television. ABC, for example, broadcast 12 stories on Bosnia in May, 14 stories in June, and 60 in the final six months of 1992. One must go back to April, then, to see what impact television had in getting Bosnia onto the foreign-policy agenda in the United States.

The war in Bosnia emerged as a major issue in Washington on April 7, when the Bush administration granted diplomatic recognition to the

---

[63] Schraeder, *Foreign Policy toward Africa*, pp. 177–78.

newly independent states of Bosnia, Croatia, and Slovenia. As of April 7, not one story on Bosnia had appeared on the major networks in 1992.[64] NBC broadcast a story on Bosnia on April 7, and CBS on April 13, but not until April 19–25 (when six stories on Bosnia appeared on the evening news) does Bosnia emerge as a major focus of the evening news.

The fighting in Bosnia, however, had been raging for weeks. The *New York Times* reported on March 15 that "tensions [in Bosnia] reached a new high with rival ethnic groups setting up barricades in the center of Sarajevo. At least a dozen people were killed."[65] On March 19 the *New York Times* reported "a dangerous rise in ethnic tensions" in Bosnia,[66] and on April 6 it described the violence in Bosnia as "the worst since World War II."[67] The war in Bosnia, in other words, had not erupted suddenly on April 7, although on American television it appeared to have done just that.

As of April 19, when the first cluster of Bosnia stories on the evening news begins—just two had appeared in 1992 up to this point—Washington had demonstrated great interest in the conflict. On April 14, Secretary of State James Baker described the situation in Bosnia as "extraordinarily tragic."[68] On April 15 the State Department declared Serbian actions in Bosnia to be "completely outside the bounds of civilized behavior" and warned that Serbia could "very quickly become an international pariah."[69] A Bush administration official told the *New York Times* on April 16 that in recognizing Bosnia, "We want to put a marker down to the Serbs and make our point," leading the *Times* to conclude: "it is now clear that Mr. Baker wants the United States to play a prominent part in dealing with Serbia and the Bosnian crisis."[70] Four days later the *New York Times* would describe Baker as "deeply engaged" in the conflict in the former Yugoslavia.[71] The Bush administration, in other words, had made clear its own sense of the magnitude of the Bosnian crisis *before* television made it into a major story.

---

[64] As in the Somalia case, I set aside brief studio reports, which are clearly not what those who see television as setting the foreign-policy agenda have in mind.

[65] John F. Burns, "U.N. Peacekeeping Force Moves into Yugoslavia," *New York Times*, March 15, 1992, p. 6.

[66] Chuck Sudetic, "Yugoslav Groups Reach an Accord," *New York Times*, March 19, 1992, A9.

[67] Chuck Sudetic, "Ethnic Clashes Increase in Bosnia as Europe Recognition Vote Nears," *New York Times*, April 6, 1992, A12.

[68] Chuck Sudetic, "Breaking Cease-Fire, Serbs Launch Attacks into Bosnia," *New York Times*, April 15, 1992, A6.

[69] "Halt Fighting in Bosnia, U.S. Warns Serbia, *Chicago Tribune*, April 16, 1992, p. 3.

[70] David Binder, "U.S. Sends Envoy to Bosnia as Part of Wider Campaign," *New York Times*, April 17, 1992, A8.

[71] David Binder, "Baker Weighing a Break with Belgrade," *New York Times*, April 21, 1992, A3.

Once it had taken an interest in the story, television news presented the American response to the war in Bosnia in quite critical terms, focusing on the failure of the United States to act. For example:

"Once, the world cared about ethnic or ideological disputes in the Balkans. . . . So far, Bosnia-Herzegovina has been given mainly moral support from the outside world. If it is to survive in the coming weeks, it will need more than that" (ABC, April 19).

"But all the diplomacy in Washington and across Europe amounts to little more than scolding the Serbs and is having no visible impact on their behavior" (ABC, May 12).

"Today's vote [at the U.N. to impose sanctions on Serbia] follows months of indecision and inaction on the part of the United States" (ABC, May 30).

"On this spot the peace-loving nations of the world did nothing" (Text of cartoon, ABC, June 25).[72]

The clear implication of these stories is that the United States could have done more to stop the fighting in Bosnia. It turns out, however, that the Bush administration itself had done much to encourage this interpretation.

In the military interventions examined in chapters 3, 4, and 5 (except for the Somalia case in chapter 5), the White House made a concerted effort to explain and win support for its actions, offering the media a simple story and a tangible policy to report. The United States invaded Grenada to counter the expansion of Communism and to protect American lives; sent troops to Saudi Arabia to resist an act of "naked aggression"; bombed Libya to retaliate against terrorism; and so on. In the case of Bosnia, however, journalists found no evidence that the United States *had a policy* to speak of. Despite this, the Bush administration made public statements expressing great concern about Bosnia. It called attention to the crisis but then seemed to have no idea how to deal with it.

On May 5, the Bush administration itself offered this analysis. A State Department official explained to the *New York Times* that the United States had no effective policy on Bosnia: "After assuming a leading role in trying to defuse the Yugoslav conflict three weeks ago, the Bush administration has largely withdrawn from the issue 'in anger and frustration,' a senior Administration official has said."[73] But the television coverage continued. Having illuminated the crisis in Bosnia, the White House could not return it to obscurity. It is hard to imagine a scenario more likely to inspire journalists to report "months of indecision and inaction on the part of the United States" than one where the White House declares some-

---

[72] *World News Tonight* (dates as indicated).

[73] David Binder, "U.S., Frustrated, Backs Off from the Crisis in Yugoslavia," *New York Times*, May 5, 1992, A10.

thing to be a major international crisis, tries to do something about it, and then explains that it has backed off in "anger and frustration." Television news in the spring of 1992 did not criticize a policy that had been formulated, implemented, and explained. It simply observed that no such policy existed.[74]

Congress also started to question U.S. policy toward Bosnia. As of May 15, members of Congress had declined to speak out on the issue, enabling the *New York Times* to report: "In Congress, there is virtually no demand for action" on Bosnia. As a congressional aide explained, "No one really has any good ideas."[75] Congress would soon get some ideas, of course; the *New York Times* reported in June that "Republican and Democratic Senators are pressing the Bush Administration to consider military intervention to end the siege of Sarajevo."[76] It is interesting to note, however, that because the Bush administration had set goals that it then failed to achieve and abandoned, ABC had been quite critical of the U.S. response to the crisis in Bosnia even before much opposition had been expressed in Congress.

As the war in Bosnia continued, the Bush and Clinton administrations made periodic expressions of outrage and mounted a series of efforts to do something to end the conflict. Until 1995, however, these efforts were a manifest failure. Each effort, moreover, generated opposition in Congress, some members demanding more aggressive action, others warning against U.S. intervention. Bush and Clinton would then step back and reassess their policies. It is therefore no surprise to find that media coverage of the American response to the crisis in Bosnia often had a critical tone. When U.S. policy is not well defined, manifestly unsuccessful, and denounced in Congress, journalists do point this out.

The Case of the Iraqi Kurds

As March turned to April in the spring of 1991, television news made the ill-fated rebellion of the Iraqi Kurds against the regime of Saddam Hussein a major story in the United States. The spirit of much of this coverage is captured in ABC's report on April 1:

---

[74] This is consistent with Strobel's conclusion that the media have influenced U.S. foreign policy in the 1990s "when that policy was weakly held, when it was in flux, or when it did not have congressional and public support. If policymakers are inattentive or unsure, then someone else will determine the direction. When policy is clear and strongly held by the executive branch, is communicated well, and has congressional and public backing, the news media tend to follow." See Warren P. Strobel, *Late-Breaking Foreign Policy: The News Media's Influence on Peace Operations* (Washington: United States Institute of Peace Press, 1997), p. 9.

[75] Barbara Crossette, "Failure of the New Order," *New York Times*, May 15, 1992, A1.

[76] "U.N. Convoy Is Attacked on Edge of Sarajevo as More Units Arrive," *New York Times*, June 11, 1992, A6.

Saddam Hussein may finally have succeeded in breaking the back of the rebellion against him. . . . [I]t is clear tonight that without the American support they had in some cases begged for, the Kurds will not prevail.[77]

The evening news reported the plight of the Iraqi Kurds in poignant terms and pointed out the failure of the Bush administration to act on their behalf. Although Washington had declined at first to respond to Kurdish pleas, when the flight of thousands of refugees from Iraqi government forces made it onto the evening news in early April, the Bush administration imposed a no-fly zone over northern Iraq, commenced an airlift of humanitarian aid, and on April 16 announced that U.S. troops would be sent to northern Iraq to aid Kurdish refugees.[78] Strobel describes television coverage of northern Iraq as "critical to Bush's policy switch."[79] As there is no evidence of significant criticism in Congress of U.S. inaction before the story appeared on television at the end of March, this might be a case of independent media influence on U.S. foreign policy.

An examination of White House actions *before* the Iraqi Kurds made the news, however, indicates that the Bush administration itself had made a major contribution to the framing of the crisis as one the United States could do something about.[80] On February 15, President Bush declared— in reference to the future of Saddam Hussein—that the Iraqi people should "take matters into their own hands to force Saddam Hussein, the dictator, to step aside."[81] On March 1, the president told reporters: "In my own view I've always said that it would be, that the Iraqi people should put him aside, and that would facilitate the resolution of all these problems that exist."[82] As Iraqi forces moved to suppress the Kurdish insurgency in the north, the White House indicated that Iraq's use of helicopters against the Kurds violated the terms of the Gulf War cease-fire.[83] Bush stated on March 13, "I must confess to some concern about the use of Iraqi helicopters in violation of what our understanding was,"[84] and told reporters (also on March 13) that he was issuing a "warning" to Iraq: "Do not do this."[85]

---

[77] *World News Tonight*, April 1, 1991.

[78] See Strobel, *Late-Breaking Foreign Policy*, pp. 127–31.

[79] Ibid., p. 128.

[80] Strobel makes this point (ibid., p. 217).

[81] "Excerpts from 2 Statements by Bush on Iraq's Proposal for Ending Conflict," *New York Times*, February 16, 1991, p. 5.

[82] "Excerpts from Bush's News Conference on Postwar Plans," *New York Times*, March 2, 1991, p. 5.

[83] Jonathan C. Randal and Valerie Strauss, "Rebels Said to Control Much of Northern Iraq," *Washington Post*, March 15, 1991, A37.

[84] *Nightline*, March 13, 1991.

[85] David Lauter and John M. Broder, "U.S. Insists It Won't Meddle in Iraqi Uprisings," *Los Angeles Times*, March 27, 1991, A1.

Seen in this context, the decision of journalists to frame the suppression of the Kurds as something the United States could have prevented appears to be a logical response to the White House reaction to the crisis. The president first encouraged Iraqis to overthrow their government and declared that Baghdad's campaign against the Kurds violated the terms of the Gulf War cease-fire. When the insurgency seemed to be on the verge of defeat, however, Washington declined to offer the assistance its words had encouraged the insurgents to expect.[86] As it had done on Bosnia, the White House spoke out on a conflict and warned one side to back off, but failed to formulate a policy that could achieve this objective.

Contradictions in American policy, of course, do not always result in critical coverage. When Iraq invaded Kuwait, the White House suddenly changed its position on Saddam Hussein, a contradiction journalists (as a rule) declined to report.[87] The reason the contradiction went unreported, however, is not hard to see. In August, the Bush administration conducted a massive, orchestrated campaign—unopposed in Washington—to explain its new position on Iraq, and this dominated the news. But in March, the Bush administration offered an ambiguous policy—first warning Iraq that it could not use its helicopters against the Kurds, then declining to enforce its warning—and made no real effort to sell the policy, as it had in August. The blunt assessment of the *Financial Times* is representative of the view of most journalists in March: "U.S. objectives are confused."[88]

American policy in August, moreover, had succeeded in its stated objective of defending Saudi Arabia. U.S. policy in March manifestly failed, until the no-fly zone was declared, as Iraq declined to heed American warnings. The case of the Iraqi Kurds indicates that when the White House offers a contradictory policy and makes no real effort to sell it, and the policy fails, journalists note the contradictions and report the failure. The American media are not simply a propaganda instrument of the U.S. government, even when White House policies are unopposed in Washington. When the president fails to articulate a clear policy and the ambiguous policy that emerges to fill the vacuum does not work, journalists report this, even if opposition party politicians in Washington do not speak out. But if this is the best evidence that can be offered on behalf of the independence of the American media, one must conclude that the prevailing definition of independence is not a very demanding one.

[86] William Safire, "Bush's Bay of Pigs," *New York Times*, April 4, 1991, A23.
[87] Dorman and Livingston, "News and Historical Content."
[88] Peter Riddell, "Anguish of Victory," *Financial Times*, March 30, 1991, p. 7.

Seven

Conclusion

IN THEIR coverage of U.S. intervention in the post-Vietnam era, the *New York Times, World News Tonight,* and the *MacNeil/Lehrer Newshour* have made no independent contribution (except at the margins) to foreign-policy debate in the United States. The spectrum of debate in Washington, instead, has determined the spectrum of debate in the news. The evidence supports not just the correlation version of the indexing hypothesis, but the marginalization version. Coverage of critical viewpoints on U.S. interventions does not increase from a reasonable baseline in the news when U.S. policy generates conflict in Washington, but is marginalized in the news when official actors are united (see table 5.1 for an overview of the evidence). The evidence also shows that journalists could have reported critical perspectives in the Washington consensus cases, if foreign-policy experts outside of Washington and interested, engaged citizens had been consulted. Here I offer some concluding observations on the relationship of the journalism described in this book to the First Amendment ideal of a press independent of government, some prescriptions for independent journalism, and some reflections on the impact of the news on U.S. foreign policy.

Neither a Watchdog Nor a Mirror

Under one model of an independent press, the press is independent of government if journalists are free to report criticism of public officials and their policies. American journalists have this freedom. But what has been done with it in practice? In assessing the independence of the American media, this is the fundamental question that must be addressed.

If critical viewpoints on U.S. foreign policy are not reported in the news unless they have been expressed inside the government first, then in practice the press is independent of the *president,* but not the *government.* When Potter Stewart writes that the First Amendment establishes "a fourth institution outside the Government as an additional check on the three official branches,"[1] and Hugo Black declares that in the First Amend-

---

[1] Quoted in Bollinger, *Images of Free Press,* p. 177, n. 44.

ment "The Government's power to censor the press was abolished so that the press would remain forever free to censure the Government,"[2] there is no indication that "the Government" the Justices speak of is just the White House, and that Congress is to be understood as a vantage point "outside the Government." Journalism that uses the indexing rule to set the spectrum of debate in the news, however, must rest its claim to independence on this strange premise.

The job of an independent press is not just to report the words and deeds of official actors, but to offer a perspective based "outside the Government." Journalists who grant to politicians the power to set the spectrum of debate in the news, I have argued, are abdicating their place in the American constitutional regime. Their independence exists in principle, but does not manifest itself in practice.

There is one possible objection to the argument that should be addressed. It could be said that viewpoints and perspectives are something *news* media are not in the business of reporting. This claim does not speak to the *New York Times* opinion pages and the *MacNeil/Lehrer Newshour*, but it could be made for the *New York Times* news section and *World News Tonight*. The news section and the evening news, some have asserted, simply "report the news" and are not designed to report viewpoints and perspectives.[3]

The news does contain tangible facts. When the United States invaded Panama, for example, troops, tanks, and planes went into action. Noriega vanished, fires blazed, civilians died, and a world of other facts were there to be reported. But tangible facts are just one aspect of the story. To President Bush, the heart of the story went something like this: the United States liberated Panama from an oppressive dictator and shut down a major arm of the international drug trade. To opponents of U.S. policy, the heart of the story was that the United States violated international law to punish a disloyal client. In telling the story, each side calls attention to those facts that support its own version of what happened. Because of the contradictions between the two versions of the story, efforts to simply "report the news," free of viewpoint and perspective, are bound to fail, unless the words of each source could somehow be filtered to extract the elements of interpretation and perspective. But this is not possible, for as one reporter said to Gans: "we don't deal in facts but in attributed opinions."[4] When government officials explain U.S. foreign policy and others critique it, their facts are a function of their perspective. Fact and opinion merge

[2] Quoted in Hentoff, *The First Freedom,* p. 206.
[3] Paletz, "Just Deserts?" p. 280.
[4] Gans, *Deciding What's News,* p. 130.

in explanations of U.S. foreign policy, and it is hard to imagine how one could be reported free of the other.

The reason for journalists to consult sources outside of Washington is not that their views are news. It is that sources outside of Washington balance the power of the government to establish the terms in which the story is told. The idea is to avoid defining *what happened* as *what the government says happened*. For if the source of information on American foreign policy is the U.S. government, then what is being reported is not *the* story, but *a* story, one told by a powerful interested party. Or more precisely, two powerful interested parties: Democrats and Republicans. But the fact that two parties are consulted instead of just one, the evidence in this book shows, is often much less of a difference than meets the eye.

Journalism that indexes debate in the news to debate in Washington violates not just the watchdog ideal, but also the mirror ideal. For under the indexing rule the journalistic mirror is held up not to reality, but to official interpretations of reality. Not just the watchdog idea, but the mirror ideal too is unfulfilled if the news is reported from the vantage point of the government—even a government of two parties and three branches—for this grants to government the power to determine not just the spectrum of debate on its policies in Washington, but also the basic information made available to the public in the news. Issues and alternatives that are on the Washington agenda are clearly visible in the mirror that indexing constructs, as are the clusters of facts connected to them. Issues and alternatives and related facts under discussion outside of Washington, however, go unreflected or are relegated to the mirror's edge. If the media are acting neither as a watchdog over government, nor as a mirror independent of government, then it is hard to argue that the First Amendment ideal is being fulfilled.

Prescriptions for Independent Journalism

If the problem is that journalists are letting the government set the news agenda and the spectrum of debate in the news, a simple but powerful solution would be to grant sources outside of Washington greater access to the news. Here are five rules journalist might use to achieve this objective.

1. Consult Foreign-Policy Experts outside of Washington

Experts with Washington experience offer much insight into the execution and outcome of U.S. interventions. But as a rule these experts reinforce the spectrum of foreign-policy debate inside the government. When Democrats and Republicans in Washington are in consensus, former government officials and policy-oriented Washington think tanks—products of a pragmatic foreign-policy establishment in need of "uncomplicated diagnoses and solutions in order to take action"[5]—cannot be expected to offer an independent perspective.

For a perspective independent of government, journalists could interview foreign-policy experts at universities. James A. Smith contrasts the intellectual, an ideal approximated (one hopes) in the university academic, with the inside-Washington policy expert. He observes that the intellectual,

> free of the ambition to serve a leader directly, can speak with an authority that does not need to bend the truth to justify pressing political ends. . . . The policy expert and adviser, however, if they aspire to be of use, must speak to power in a political and bureaucratic context; and they must speak a useful truth. Their claims to speak the truth must always be viewed in light of their relationship with power.[6]

As explained in chapter 2, the claim is not that university experts are wiser than inside-Washington experts, but that intellectuals and politicians perform different social functions, and that as a result of their social function politicians and Washington insiders often decline to express points of view that have substantial expert support outside of Washington.

University experts are easy to find. Journalists could contact the heads of history, political science, and other relevant departments at universities and colleges for the names of experts on specific issues, or the presidents of academic professional associations (for example, the American Historical Association or the Latin American Studies Association). In a pinch, a random sample of academic reaction could be used, just as journalists conduct random person-on-the-street interviews to get a sense of the reaction of the general public. As there are thousands of experts on U.S. foreign policy out there, television journalists could continue to favor those who perform well on their medium. In sum, journalists could continue to use their general good sense and judgment in selecting foreign-policy experts. The one requirement is that experience and reputation in Washington not be the basis of selection.

2. Report the Reaction of Engaged Citizens

Mass opinion polls offer useful information about the foreign-policy views of the general public. But if news indexed to debate in Washington is

[5] George, *Bridging the Gap*, p. 9.
[6] Smith, *The Idea Brokers*, p. xviii.

where people learn about military interventions, then mass opinion polls are not independent of Washington debate, but are to a great extent a function of it. If journalists marginalize the views of citizens who have resisted the pull of a Washington consensus based on poll numbers that are a reflection of that consensus, the independence of the press is threatened.

In reporting public opinion on U.S. foreign policy, journalists should be sure to include the reaction of interested, engaged citizens, whose relatively educated and independent (of Washington debate) views would otherwise be "submerge[d] . . . in a more apathetic mass public."[7] To get the perspective of the engaged citizen into the news, journalists could consult representatives of national public-interest organizations that speak out on U.S. foreign policy such as Peace Action (the successor to SANE/Freeze), the American Friends Service Committee, other national organizations, and the hundreds or perhaps thousands of local organizations that deal with foreign-policy issues. As such organizations are eager for media attention, reporters would have no problem tracking them down. Journalists should of course be careful not to favor public-interest organizations on either side of the political spectrum, but should report the views of a representative (at an approximation) sample of organized opinion.

Concern about granting bizarre or paranoid perspectives access to the news would be easy to address. A conservative rule of thumb—but one that would have been effective in expanding the spectrum of debate in the cases examined in this book—would be to double-check the views of public-interest organizations with outside-Washington foreign-policy experts, to screen out absurd claims such as the supposed United Nations invasion of America with black helicopters. The experts would not have to *endorse* the perspective of a citizen organization, but would simply establish that it met a minimal threshold of plausibility. The arguments of engaged citizens discussed in chapters 3 and 4 would get past this hurdle with ease. The same end could be achieved with the exercise of basic journalistic common sense.

In their abstract rhetoric, journalists elevate the public to an exalted place in the democratic system. In practice, journalists need to realize that there are often more sides to "public opinion" than what mass opinion polls and the person-on-the-street interview reveal. The engaged citizen also deserves a hearing, not as a critic of government policy per se, but as a manifestation of "public opinion" that is independent of Washington debate.

---

[7] Ginsberg, "Polling Transforms Public Opinion," p. 276.

3. Expand Critical Analysis of the Execution of U.S. Policy to Encompass the Policy Itself

American journalists do a great job of evaluating the execution of U.S. foreign policy. The problem described in this book would disappear if a similar critical zeal were devoted to examining its wisdom and justification. In consulting foreign-policy experts and engaged citizens outside of Washington, it is essential that journalists not let questions of execution crowd out questions of policy when there is consensus inside the government.

If it sounds unrealistic or utopian to expect the news media to offer critical analysis of the wisdom and justification of foreign-policy decisions, chapters 3, 4, and 5 demonstrate that when foreign-policy decisions are questioned in Washington, their wisdom and justification is the subject of extensive debate in the news. A press independent of government would not let official actors decide when critical analysis of government policy is to be reported. In interviewing sources outside of Washington, journalists must be sure to let them speak about U.S. policy itself, not marginalize such reaction with a series of execution-oriented questions.

4. Expand the Spectrum of Foreign-Policy Debate without Increasing Strategy Coverage

One possible response to the critique of the press in this book would be for journalists to increase their reporting on the strategic calculations that structure Washington debate. When Democrats declined to criticize U.S. intervention in Panama and the Persian Gulf, journalists could have explained the political logic behind their decision.

The problem with this solution is that more analysis of the motives and strategies of politicians—such as pervades election coverage and the Washington political beat, but not foreign-policy coverage—would exacerbate public cynicism about politicians and politics. Research on election coverage has demonstrated that in framing American politics as a strategic contest for power, as opposed to a system for dealing with issues of public concern, the press has encouraged cynicism and disengagement in the public.[8] News that examined the political motives behind foreign-policy debate in Washington would therefore come at a significant cost to the public sphere. Rather than expanding their focus on the strategic calculations of politicians into foreign-policy coverage, journalists should just

---

[8] See Cappella and Jamieson, *Spiral of Cynicism*.

stop letting those calculations set the news agenda and the spectrum of debate in the news. The idea is for the news to be independent of the strategic calculations of politicians, not for the attention of the public to be focused on those calculations.

5. Report Outside-Washington Perspectives in Lead Stories

On those rare occasions where opposition outside of Washington to a bipartisan foreign-policy consensus is reported, it tends to be in stories on the inside pages, often stories that focus on protest as a social phenomenon, examining the behavior and the motives of the protesters as much as their message (see chapter 5). It is the lead news stories, however, that have the power to define and interpret events for the causal reader/viewer. If coverage of outside-Washington perspectives on U.S. foreign policy is essential to the realization of the First Amendment ideal, it should not be relegated to the margins of the news, but included in the lead stories that are the heart of the coverage.

Some would argue that foreign-policy news is not going to improve without fundamental reform of the American media system. Corporate ownership of the media is often said to block the realization of journalistic ideals. Corporate owners put pressure on news organizations to increase their profits, often slashing budgets and staff.[9] If journalists gravitate toward official sources because of the need to minimize their expenditure of time and money, as I argued in chapter 2, increased corporate ownership of the media might be expected to produce increased reliance on official sources.

To be realistic, prescriptions for greater journalistic independence must recognize the economic realities of the news business. The reforms I have suggested would not require journalists to embark upon time-consuming and expensive investigative ventures, but simply to expand their pools of expert and citizen sources. This should entail just a marginal increase in the expenditure of journalistic time and corporate money. Budget-cutting corporate owners, although not helpful to the cause of reform, should not preclude its implementation.

There is also the concern that corporate owners shade news stories to serve their economic and ideological interests. Corporate interests in U.S. foreign policy are substantial. But while there is a solid foundation to these

[9] See Erik Barnouw et al., *Conglomerates and the Media* (New York: New Press, 1997), especially chapters by Richard M. Cohen and Gene Roberts; and Ben H. Bagdikian, *The Media Monopoly* (Boston: Beacon Press, 1997).

concerns,[10] American journalists do have some real editorial freedom within the corporation. One reason for this is the self-interest of the corporate owner: if a news organization turned into a genuine propaganda organ for the parent corporation, it would lose its credibility, and the impact of the corporate message would be negated. The rational corporate owner therefore strikes a balance between the temptation to dictate the content of the news and the need to preserve its credibility with journalists and the public. If journalists decided to step outside of the indexing rule in the name of the First Amendment ideal, the corporation would be hard pressed to demand that it be reimposed without threatening this delicate balance.

Or perhaps such a demand *would* be made. If journalists endeavored to put into practice the changes suggested here, and corporate ownership vetoed the changes, we would have evidence that structural reform of the American media system is required before the problem of indexing can be addressed. But until there is evidence that journalists have in fact *tried* to get beyond the indexing rule in their foreign-policy reporting, the concern that change might not be possible within the existing media system remains a theoretical one.

Domestic Politics and Foreign Policy

If change is needed for the press to achieve the First Amendment ideal, and if it is realistic to imagine that such change could be implemented in practice, what would be the implications for U.S. foreign policy? One might expect evidence that the media make no independent contribution to foreign-policy debate to be welcome news to those in the classical realist tradition of foreign-policy analysis (thinkers such as Hans Morgenthau and George Kennan).[11] Classical realism asserts that foreign policy should be made by enlightened statesmen, attuned to the national interest, and free of the impact of extraneous domestic factors such as the news media. Neorealism, a variation on classical realism, claims that foreign policy *is* made free of the influence of domestic factors.[12] The conventional wisdom is that evidence of the impact of the media on foreign-policy debate is evidence of the influence of domestic factors on foreign policy. If the media in fact do *not* have an independent impact, this might seem to support the realist position.

[10] Bagdikian, *The Media Monopoly.*

[11] George F. Kennan, *American Diplomacy, 1900–1950* (Chicago: University of Chicago Press, 1951); Hans J. Morganthau, *Politics among Nations* (New York: Knopf, 1948).

[12] On neorealism see Robert O. Keohane, ed., *Neorealism and Its Critics* (New York: Columbia University Press, 1986).

Such an inference would be incorrect. The reason the media have no independent impact on foreign-policy debate is that journalists have ceded to *politicians* the power to set the spectrum of debate in the news. The indexing rule therefore enables a major factor that realists see as extraneous to sound foreign policy—*domestic politics*—to structure foreign-policy debate in the public sphere. The independent impact of the media on foreign-policy debate is marginal, but the impact of domestic politics turns out to be quite strong. The agenda-setting power journalists decline to exercise does not vanish into the air. Instead, it is passed on to politicians.

What this means is that if the news influences public opinion, and if presidents weigh public opinion in their foreign-policy decisions, journalism that went beyond the indexing rule would counter the influence of domestic politics on U.S. foreign policy. A press independent of government would grant more influence to sources outside of Washington who are free of its politics, sources one might expect to be better attuned than politicians to the elements of an enlightened and realistic foreign policy, and less inclined to "play politics" in their foreign-policy prescriptions. Evidence supporting the indexing hypothesis should *not* be pleasing to realists, as it indicates that the news encourages presidents to respond to domestic political imperatives, instead of the realities of the international environment as interpreted outside of Washington.

While the strategic decisions of the Democratic Party produced near-unanimous support in Washington for the Panama invasion and U.S. intervention in the Persian Gulf (except in November), outside of Washington interpretations of the national interest were more diverse. The national interest might well have been better served if Washington politics—where certain alternatives had been "organized out" of foreign-policy debate for reasons unrelated to an evaluation of their substantive merits—had not had so great an influence on foreign-policy news.[13] Independent journalism could have reduced the impact of politics on foreign-policy debate in the public sphere.

One need not be a realist to be critical of the journalism I have described. My point here is not to endorse either classical realism or neorealism, but simply to observe that evidence supporting the indexing hypothesis does *not* mean the news media have no impact on U.S. foreign policy. Under the indexing rule, the impact of the media is to reinforce the spectrum of debate Washington politics has produced, and to exclude from

[13] Some realists have in fact criticized the invasion of Panama and the Gulf War, arguing that U.S. interests in each case would have been better served if military force had not been used. See Tucker and Hendrickson, *The Imperial Temptation*, pp. 46–47 on Panama, pp. 73–162 on the Gulf War.

the public sphere perspectives that do not have political support inside the government. If one believes that political calculations often fail to produce sound foreign policies, this impact must be judged to be negative.

The Question of Governing

In the end there is the question of governing. Perhaps news media that are not independent players in the construction of foreign-policy debate serve the interest of the nation in having an effective president. Setting the public agenda and the terms of public debate are major aspects of the president's job, and to the extent that journalists defer to Washington on such matters, the job of the president is made easier. If the choice were one between an independent press and an effective government, defenders of indexing would have a powerful argument on their side.

Governments need agendas in order to govern, and the journalism de-scribed in this book does increase the power of the government to set the public agenda. But independent journalism is not at odds with effective government. News indexed to debate in Washington does make it easier for presidents to do what the political logic of the moment appears to prescribe, as policies that win bipartisan support in Washington also get positive media coverage. But what seems at first to be effective governing often contributes to a governing crisis down the road.

The great example of this in U.S. foreign policy is Vietnam. When Lyndon Johnson escalated the war in Vietnam in 1965, convinced that if he acted otherwise he would be committing political suicide as the presi-dent who "lost Vietnam," supportive news coverage paved the way.[14] In the judgment of history, however, the Johnson administration erred to the extent that it let political calculations influence U.S. foreign policy, instead of offering the leadership that might have enabled the United States to get out of Vietnam and focus its energies on other objectives. In 1965, supportive coverage inside the terms of the Washington consensus made it easy for Johnson to govern. But by 1968, the ramifications of the decision made in 1965 had made effective governing impossible. To the extent that the media had an impact on Johnson's decision—and it is clear that Johnson was very interested in how his Vietnam policies were re-ported[15]—it would have been to encourage a decision that would lead to a governing crisis.

Although neither the Panama invasion nor the Gulf War had the monu-mental impact on the United States of Vietnam, politicians of the post–

[14] Hallin, *The "Uncensored War."*
[15] Ibid., pp. 62, 108.

Cold War era could end up in a governing crisis if the U.S. defense budget continues to be maintained at near–Cold War dimensions, at the expense of funding for other foreign and domestic needs.[16] But the political logic of the 1990s has discouraged major defense cuts. One party counts supporters of defense spending as its core constituents, and the other continues to fear charges of softness on defense, producing a consensus on the need to maintain Cold War levels of defense spending. The Panama invasion and the Gulf War—said to be evidence of the continued utility of military force—contributed much to the emergence of this consensus.

Media coverage of the Panama invasion and the Gulf War reinforced the consensus politics had produced, enabling the White House to determine the framing of its policies in the public sphere. Figures outside of Washington interested in reshaping the debate on military and defense issues could not get their message out--a message that might have made it easier for politicians to govern down the road if funding for nondefense programs continues to be elusive.[17]

Governing sometimes requires acts of innovative leadership that transcend what immediate political calculations appear to prescribe. This is why presidents who seem to be "playing politics" in their conduct of U.S. foreign policy are denounced. The impact of news indexed to debate in Washington, however, is to encourage policies that serve political strategies, and to discourage efforts to elevate foreign-policy debate above Washington politics.

If the First Amendment ideal could be exchanged for effective governing, a trade-off might have to be made. But if the First Amendment ideal is not just a principle to be admired, but a means to the end of effective governing, it is an ideal that journalists, as independent actors in the constitutional regime, must aspire to fulfill.

[16] The decrease in the size of the defense budget in the post–Cold War period is often exaggerated. Defense spending is well below what it had been under Reagan, but as of 1997 it could be written that "the U.S. today spends more on the military than in the years after Vietnam, when Cold War relations were still frosty. The defense budget is only barely lower than it was before the Carter-Reagan Cold War buildup. Real dollar spending in the 1990s is running about 85 percent of the Cold War average." Ann Markusen, "How We Lost the Peace Dividend," *American Prospect*, July–August 1997, p. 86.

[17] Despite the consensus in Washington, 43 percent of those polled in 1990 responded that too much was being spent on defense, against 12 percent who said the defense budget was too small. See Thomas Hartley and Bruce Russett, "Public Opinion and the Common Defense: Who Governs Military Spending in the United States?" *American Political Science Review* 86 (December 1992): 909.

Appendix

TABLE A.1
Critical Coverage in *New York Times* News Section, Washington Conflict versus
Washington Consensus

	Critical Paragraphs	Total Paragraphs	Percentage Critical
Washington Conflict			
Grenada	291	3,524	8.3
Gulf War (November)	154	1,951	7.9
Somalia	231	1,364	16.9
Haiti	127	1,784	7.1
Washington Consensus			
Libya	41	2,533	1.6
Panama	36	2,185	1.6
Gulf War (August)	60	3,756	1.6
Gulf War (January)	182	5,688	3.2

TABLE A.2
Critical Coverage on *World News Tonight*, Washington Conflict versus
Washington Consensus

	Critical Paragraphs	Total Paragraphs	Percentage Critical
Washington Conflict			
Grenada	29	323	9.0
Gulf War (November)	21	344	6.1
Somalia	18	168	10.7
Haiti	28	293	9.6
Washington Consensus			
Libya	6	340	1.8
Panama	4	271	1.5
Gulf War (August)	3	856	0.4
Gulf War (January)	47	1,940	2.4

TABLE A.3
Critical *New York Times* Editorials and Columns, Washington Conflict versus
Washington Consensus

	Critical Editorials/ Columns	Total Editorials/ Columns	Percentage Critical
Washington Conflict			
Grenada	12	27	44
Gulf War (November)	10	29	34
Somalia	6	9	67
Haiti	7	18	39
Washington Consensus			
Libya	7	24	29
Panama	2	15	13
Gulf War (August)	1	38	3
Gulf War (January)	7	58	12

TABLE A.4
Critical *MacNeil/Lehrer Newshour* Guests, Washington Conflict versus
Washington Consensus

	Critical Guests	Total Guests	Percentage Critical
Washington Conflict			
Grenada	7	18	39
Gulf War (November)	10	27	37
Somalia	11	28	39
Haiti	4	18	22
Washington Consensus			
Libya	6	17	35
Panama	0	17	0
Gulf War (August)	4	70	6
Gulf War (January)	2	46	4

v

Index

Latin America, 48, 50, 52–53, 60n, 104, 106

Latin American Studies Association, 146

Lebanon, 12, 61, 69, 96

Lehrer, Jim, 113

letters to the editor. *See* public opinion

Lewis, Anthony, 113–14

Lewis, Flora, 105

Lewis, John, 135–36

LEXIS/NEXIS, 57, 85, 133

Libya, U.S. bombing of, 3, 5, 12, 15, 43, 51, 100–8, 111, 114, 139; French denial of airspace, 103, 104, 107n, 119; and Western hostages, 106–7

Lieberman, Joseph, 129

Livingston, Steven, 20, 127n, 129n

Long Island Alliance for Peaceful Alternatives, 84

Los Angeles Coalition Against U.S. Intervention in the Middle East, 84

Los Angeles Times, 103, 104

Lowenthal, Abraham F., 38, 40

Luttwak, Edward, 96

MacNeil/Lehrer Newshour, 14–15, 42, 44, 144; and the buildup to the Gulf War, 73, 75–76, 80–81, 83, 96; evidence summarized, 100–1, 107, 143, 155; and Grenada, 51; guests on U.S. intervention, 31, 34; and the Gulf War, 107, 113; and Haiti, 119; and Libya, 100–1, 103, 105, 106–7, 119; and Panama, 51; and Somalia (1993), 115; as a test of the indexing hypothesis, 12–13, 31

Maine, 79

Mandelbaum, Michael, 120

Marcham, Jane, 83

McCain, John, 71, 72, 117

McConnell, Mitch, 129

McGovern, George, 71

McWethy, John, 78

Mediterranean Sea, 91, 103

Mexico, 39, 52, 53, 70

Miller, Joe, 111

Millett, Richard, 58

mirror ideal, 23–24, 27, 145

Mitchell, George, 66, 95

Mondale, Walter, 41, 62, 63

Morgenthau, Hans, 150

Moynihan, Daniel Patrick, 41, 46, 67, 94

Mueller, John, 80n

Nairobi, 135

National Football League, 58

National Journal, 63

NATO. *See* European allies

NBC Nightly News, 117, 122–24, 128, 131–38

Netherlands, 104

Neuman, W. Russell, 33

New York, 48

New York Times, 15, 16, 18n, 42, 44, 67–68, 88, 144; and Bosnia, 138–40; and the buildup to the Gulf War, 68–77, 79, 80, 92–96, 97; evidence summarized, 100–1, 107, 143, 154, 155; and Grenada, 45–52, 61–62; and the Gulf War, 45, 101, 107–14, 119; and Haiti, 119; influence of, xi, 12–13; as a liberal paper, 13; and Libya, 43, 100–7, 119; and Panama, 39, 45, 48–53, 55–56, 60; and Somalia (1992), 135; and Somalia (1993), 101, 115–17

news sources: business, 28–29; foreign, 13–14, 15, 51–53, 68, 73–74, 105; foreign policy experts as, 11, 28–32, 33n, 35, 57–59, 76, 84–86, 99, 112–13, 143, 145–46, 148, 149,; former government officials as, 28–31, 57, 146; interest groups as, 28; official, 8–9, 11, 17–19, 28, 43, 47, 48, 75, 117, 121, 131, 149; person-on-the-street as, 11, 32, 69–70, 71, 94, 108–10, 112, 113, 146, 147; presumed credibility of, 18–19; think tanks as, 28–31, 57, 146; university academics as, 28, 30–31, 57–58, 65, 85, 106, 146, 147; with a special interest, 69, 70, 72, 75. *See also* public opinion, engaged citizens and; public opinion, in public interest organizations

Nicaragua, 5, 10, 22, 52, 53

Nixon, Richard, 4, 32, 48

Noriega, Manuel, 3, 38–40, 43n, 48, 50, 53–56, 58, 60, 61, 63, 78, 144

North American Free Trade Area, 135

North Carolina, 72, 110

Nunn, Sam, 41, 67, 88, 89, 92, 94, 117

O'Neill, Tip, 41, 42, 47, 62

OPEC, 70

Organization of American States, 38

Organization of East Caribbean States, 40, 46